RENEWING
YOUR
MIND

IDENTITY AND THE MATTER OF CHOICE

DENNIS JERNIGAN

Published by Innovo Publishing, LLC
www.innovopublishing.com
1-888-546-2111

Providing Full-Service Publishing Services for Christian Authors, Artists & Organizations:
Hardbacks, Paperbacks, eBooks, Audiobooks, Music & Film

RENEWING YOUR MIND:
IDENTITY AND THE MATTER OF CHOICE

Unless otherwise noted, all scripture is taken from the *New American Standard Bible®*, Copyright © 1960,1962,1963,1968,1971,1972,1973,1975,1977,1995 by The Lockman Foundation. Used by permission.

Scripture quotations marked (*NIV*) are taken from *The Holy Bible, New International Version®*, NIV® Copyright © 1973, 1978, 1984, 2011 by Biblica, Inc.® Used by permission. All rights reserved worldwide.

Scripture quotations marked (*NLT*) are taken from *The Holy Bible, New Living Translation,* Copyright © 1996, 2004, 2007 by Tyndale House Foundation. Used by permission of Tyndale House Publishers, Inc., Carol Stream, Illinois 60188. All rights reserved.

Scripture quotations marked (*TM*) are taken from *The Message*. Copyright © 1993, 1994, 1995, 1996, 2000, 2001, 2002. Used by permission of NavPress Publishing Group.

Scripture quotations marked (*NKJV*) are taken from *The Holy Bible, New King James Version®*. Copyright © 1982 by Thomas Nelson. Used by permission.

Library of Congress Control Number: 2017945597
ISBN: 978-1-61314-373-5

Cover Design & Interior Layout: Innovo Publishing, LLC

Printed in the United States of America
U.S. Printing History
First Edition: October 2017

ENDORSEMENTS

"I've had the blessed opportunity to minister with many godly and anointed people in my life time. But I have never met or stood alongside someone with the uniqueness of gifting, calling, and spirit as Dennis. His ability to live and manifest Father's love had my jaw on the ground so many times I lost count. The love of God saved him, healed him, and now flows through him in such undeniable ways. It is an honor to know him and was such a blessing to experience the power of that love first hand. Renewing Your Mind is just another manifestation of Father's love flowing through Dennis. This book is not another mind lesson, or technique in behavior modification. Rather it's filled with the life of someone who has obviously walked with the Master, been filled with His love, and had the power of His Word transform his life. I love that this is not just another man's opinion on what you should do. But rather, it's a road map and journey through Father's Word on a course to health and healing. The church is filled with wounded individuals, and this book is an excellent tool for the Holy Spirit to use in the "implantation of the Word for the healing of the soul" (Ja. 1:21). Dennis is a seeker. And I love the precious truths Father let him find to share with us all."
—**John Levens, Businessman, Ft. Worth, Texas**

"Dennis Jernigan's new book, Renewing Your Mind, is a miracle of wisdom and brevity. It is fearless, yet simple; approachable, yet transforming. It pulls no punches, yet every word is a balm of grace and hope. Having known Dennis for many years, I know how deeply he cares for those trapped in gender confusion. I also know the remarkable freedom he embodies in his own life and is therefore uniquely qualified to impart to others. Renewing Your Mind is practical sanctification at its finest—a truth bomb of great frankness, candor, and insight that can truly liberate your soul. Many miracle stories are about to be told and retold by those who read this book."
—**Dean Briggs, author of *Ekklesia Rising, Consumed,* and *The Legends of Karac Tor,* Kansas City, MO**

"Dennis Jernigan's latest book, Renewing Your Mind, is a symphony of love from a heart that has been transformed by Jesus Christ! In our broken world, we are too often influenced by secular culture's false constructs of outward beauty, pleasure, power, and success. In Jernigan's book, he reminds us of the important truth of who God says we are and how we can renew our minds to embrace an identity as a child of a loving heavenly Father! Through his own personal trials of overcoming brokenness and pain, Jernigan's wisdom shines through in his inspirational story of healing. Both practical and spiritually rich, Renewing Your Mind is a must-read for Christians seeking hope and healing for sexual and relational brokenness!"

—**Christopher Doyle, MA, LPC, LCPC, Executive Director of the Institute for Healthy Families, Author of *The Meaning of Sex: A New Christian Ethos***

PREFACE

My struggles were born of my confusion over my identity. This confusion resulted in chaotic thinking in regard to my sexuality. Before you proceed in reading this book, bear in mind that due to my own past mental struggles concerning my identity, I receive countless requests for help in this particular area. Even if your identity struggle is not of the sexual nature, the same principles of God's Word—Truth—apply to you and your situation. It is my desire to make this book as simple as possible, yet as comprehensive as to be useful. Since I am no psychologist, I am offering only the wisdom I have gained from my experience in walking out the Truth I am trying to convey in this book. That being said, let's dive right in to my journey.

I did not want to be defined as an angry man. I did not want to be defined as a fearful man. I did not want to be defined as a homosexual. I did not want to be defined as a recovering homosexual. I did not want to be defined as an emotional basket case—yet at one time in my life, I felt all those things. I felt that those things defined me, since that was the way I felt. Feelings define no one. Feelings simply tell us what we are thinking about. If we can change the way we think, we can change the way we feel. Easier said than done, right?

Just a thought on feelings: Why in the world would anyone allow the way they feel to define their entire being? I sometimes feel like lashing out in anger; yet, I don't—and I do not call myself an angry person just because I felt that way. I sometimes feel like taking something that does not belong to me; yet, I do not call myself a thief just because I felt like stealing something. I sometimes feel like a loser; yet, I do not allow that feeling to define who I am as a person.

Every feeling I have comes as a result of something I have thought. Each feeling I have is attached to a thought I have had. What I have learned is that if I change the way I think, I can change the way I feel. Some have told me I am simply brainwashing myself—and I have to agree. I have allowed Truth to wash away the lies I have thought about myself and have replaced those lies with right thinking about who and Whose I am. And guess what? My feelings have followed suit!

Don't get me wrong. This has not always been easy. It is a battle, but a battle worth fighting! Though I have fallen at times, I just keep getting back up. The only failure is the person who falls and chooses to not get back up.

I do not define myself. My Maker gets to do that. I seek Jesus. He reveals the lies I believe and shows me the Truth. It is up to me to put off those lies and to replace them with the Truth. A depth of freedom has come as a result of this mind renewal that I never thought possible. This realization keeps me seeking Jesus for more! It has afforded me something the world seems to think is impossible: self-control.

Just because something feels right doesn't mean it is, and it—that feeling—certainly does not define who I am.

> *Therefore I urge you, brethren, by the mercies of God, to present your bodies a living and holy sacrifice, acceptable to God, which is your spiritual service of worship. And do not be conformed to this world, but be transformed by the renewing of your mind, so that you may prove what the will of God is, that which is good and acceptable and perfect. (Romans 12:1-2)*

For the first twenty-two years of my life, I felt different. At first, I felt like I was something less than a real boy. I enjoyed drawing and playing the piano, and I loved dancing. My emotional sensitivity was interpreted as effeminate, and my sensitivities made the other boys uncomfortable…and I felt uncomfortable around other boys. I felt right at home with girls.

When puberty hit and sexual awareness set in, I felt as if I were something less than a man. I felt homosexual. I felt gay. That awareness—that feeling—lasted until I was twenty-two years old. At that age, something wonderful happened—or *began* to happen—that would change everything I thought about myself. What I discovered was something revolutionary and new, yet as old as time itself.

What I discovered was that I could change my feelings by simply changing the way I thought about myself—about the world in general. One of the first things that changed was my perception of homosexuality.

No longer would I think of it as my identity. After that eventful day, I began to think of it as merely a temptation—an attraction that was contrary to the way God had made me, an awareness that somewhere along the way, my thoughts concerning my sexual identity had somehow been co-opted by what I now refer to as stinkin' thinkin'.

I had believed a lie.

When one realizes they have been lied to—been duped—they feel betrayed. And I certainly felt betrayed. When one feels betrayed, they stop trusting the one who betrayed them, right? This book is my attempt to explain and express the journey toward mental and spiritual wholeness that set me free from something the world says one cannot be free of—something the world says you do not need to be free of. I wrote this book in the hope that someone else out there might be going through the same struggle I faced—regardless of whether that struggle involves their sexual identity or an addiction or a wrong belief system that leads to constant defeat—and find what they are looking for in Jesus: *the* Answer.

My desire is to operate in complete freedom—what my Maker calls freedom, rather than in what the world calls freedom: man doing what man feels like doing and calling it an identity in order to make them feel better about themselves. Feelings change according to the thoughts we think. Unless and until we deal with the underlying thoughts that lead to the feelings we have, we will never get to the root of our issues and never walk in true and real freedom, and negative feelings will rule the day. It is the man/woman who deals with their thought life—replacing lies for what is true—who walks in true freedom.

This book involves questions I have had to answer through the years that have led me from stinkin' thinkin' to right thinking; from feelings of rejection and confusion over sexual identity to feelings of knowing who and Whose I am and feelings of heterosexuality. I invite you to read on and challenge you to ask yourself the questions contained within these pages. I challenge you to see your life and identity from a Christ-centered point of view rather than from a humanistic/man-centered point of view. One leads to futility. One leads to hope. Which will you choose?

Dennis Jernigan

1

Do You Believe You Have a Choice Regarding "Whatever It Is You Are Dealing With?"

With the recent revelation from Bruce Jenner, I felt compelled to set some things, well, straight (pun intended). The gay identity was one I never wanted, and it dawned on me one day that I should seek my Maker as to what His intentions were for my identity. My plan was to choose what He called right over what my feelings—and the world—called right. I chose Truth over comfort and momentary pleasure and found freedom from my old way of thinking. In the process, I found a heterosexual identity! In a world where a man could say he was born a man but was truly a woman on the inside—and be celebrated for it—one would think a man who did not want a gay identity and found a way to a heterosexual identity would be welcomed…tolerated. But I have not found the world too open about anything other than *what feels good is right.* Choosing righteousness over license is, in this current culture, not to be tolerated. Enough about that.

People often ask me if I am still tempted with same sex attraction. When I tell them that I still understand that temptation but it no longer has power over me, their reaction is often, "Then how can you say you're changed? Nothing's different if you are still tempted." Nothing could be further from the truth.

Honestly, I had no choice in determining what would tempt me, but that in no way negates my ability to choose how I would respond to that temptation. In fact, even Jesus did not get to choose what He was tempted by—and He was tempted in *every* manner just as we are, yet without sin! We are either always creatures of choice or never creatures of choice. Our humanity has a conscience which gives us the power to choose. If we could not choose, every man would be a rapist. Every person would be obese. Every person would walk in constant anger. Every person would be hopelessly self-focused and full of pride. We *always* have a choice as to how we respond to a given situation. It just so happens that having a relationship with Christ gives us the power to overcome those temptations and to choose wisely much more easily than in our human strength! If temptation defined us, then we would succumb to the statement that "this is just who I am, so I might as well give in and *be* whatever my deepest feeling suggests I am." Temptation does not equal identity.

I did not get to choose what I was tempted by. It was just there. But it was never intended to define me. Even without Jesus, I always had the choice as to how I would respond to any given temptation, be it sexual or otherwise. Always. It was only when I allowed the temptation to define me that I began to walk in failure and allow it to control me—control my life.

I recall the look and sound and feel of temptation in that area; I am reminded of it in the media and in the culture on a daily basis (does every TV show or movie have a same sex storyline these days? Pretty much). It's in my face. But that "recalling" in no way defines who I am. Temptation is a joy. What do I mean? When temptation comes my way in *any* area that could lead me to sin, I simply ask the Holy Spirit, "What is it, Lord?" My reason is simple. The enemy—the liar, Satan—desires my downfall. Temptation is intended to lead me to that destruction. I turn to God because the temptation has become my signal that God is up to something. Why else would the enemy be after me in a certain area if not to quell the work of God in my life?

So much time has now passed since I identified as gay that it is actually difficult for me to believe I was ever that way. Of course, the liar does not want me to forget, so he continues to try and trip me up in key ways—not usually of a sexual nature, either. He attacks me in the areas of my continuing vulnerability: my sense of security or my sense of being needed or my sense of the need of affirmation—all of which are now daily met in knowing Jesus. I am now so secure that I do not fear vulnerability, nor do I fear for my security, nor do I fear that others might not think my life significant. Temptation has been relegated to use for the kingdom purposes in my life.

When it occurs, I do not allow it to determine my direction. In the moment of being tempted, temptation is now like a fly that occasionally tries to land on the meal of God's presence in my life. I shoo the pest away with the Word and continue to enjoy the feast of God's amazingly abundant presence in my life, whether I receive threats and hate from the LGBT community (and I do) or not. The temptation to fear harm is handled in the same way as sexual temptation. "What is it, Father? Your son, Dennis, waits on You…and while I wait, I will apply Your Word to my existence, bathing my being in being with you."

People can say I am not changed if I still understand temptation in my life, but for the doubters, here is a brief list off the top of my head of exactly what has changed since coming to faith in Jesus Christ:

- My belief system: I once believed I was born gay, until I was born again. I no longer believe I was ever born "that way."

- My mind: I was transformed by the renewing of my mind.

- My sexual preference: I used to be sexually aroused only by men. The sexual needs of my life are now met only by my wife, and I crave her body, by the way…

- My outlook on life: I once was depressed and self-serving. I now look toward Jesus and lay my life down for the King and for the kingdom.

I. Am. Changed. Period.

Verse:

Some call me a fool
For daring to say I've changed
But if that makes me a fool,
I wouldn't trade what I've found for anything
I'm changed
Some call me a dreamer
For daring to walk away
From my old way of thinking
My old identity now passed away
I'm changed

Chorus:

Changed from who I thought I was
Changed by pure redeeming love
Changed from death to life
And freed from every chain
Changed from old identity
Freed from lies and freed to be who my Father says I am
He calls me changed
I am changed!

Verse:

Some call me a hater for daring to disagree
Come to my own conclusion of who my Father says I am called to be
I'm changed
Some call me disillusioned
Some call it a mental break
But let there be no confusion
I am fully aware
Fully awake

And I'm changed

Chorus:

Changed from who I thought I was
Changed by pure redeeming love
Changed from death to life
And freed from every chain
Changed from old identity
Freed from lies and freed to be who my Father says I am
He calls me changed
I am changed!

---

1.   Hear the song "I Am Changed" at https://soundcloud.com/singoverme/i-am-changed-from-the-film. Words & Music: Dennis Jernigan, ©2014 Shepherd's Heart Music, Inc. www.dennisjernigan.com. To learn more about Dennis Jernigan and his story, you can purchase his autobiography, *Sing Over Me*, at http://dennisjernigan.com/store/product.php?c=26&p=3527 or watch the documentary, "Sing Over Me." The DVD is available at http://dennisjernigan.com/store/product.php?c=22&p=3572

2

The Root of the Issue

"...and you will know the truth, and the truth will make you free."
—Jesus (John 8:32)

If we are not defined by our feelings, and if we are people of choice, what does that say about our current state of feeling? How do we get to the place of not allowing our feelings to define us? Just how do we get to the place of making wise choices in spite of our feelings? As with anything in life, we get there by starting at the beginning.

When I was a boy, my family had a large garden. This garden was a main source of food for us. We canned tomatoes. We froze corn. We canned green beans. We grew potatoes and okra and carrots and radishes and anything else that might provide sustenance for our family through the winter months. It was my joy to help with that garden, at least during certain phases of said garden! It was a treat to help cut the potatoes into seed potatoes, making sure each cube of potatoes contained at least one eye. I thoroughly enjoyed the planting of the seeds because it meant that in the coming days I would experience the privilege of watching the seeds sprout and the tiny leaves breaking through the ground in search of sunshine. One of my joys was also when harvest time came. For some reason, I loved following the plow as my dad would lay the furrows over exposing mounds of ready-to-eat potatoes!

Some things about gardening I did not enjoy so much, though. One of my memories of helping with the garden was that it needed to be tended in spite of the summer's heat. Tending to that garden involved making sure pests did not ruin the plants. Going from cornstalk to cornstalk and painstakingly applying the pesticide powder was tedious. And potato bugs! My mom would pay me one penny for each potato bug I came to her with, borne in via the coffee tin she provided for the task. While fun at first, the sheer number of potato bugs seemed daunting and never ending; so numerous were the leaf-eating insects. While the tasks of applying pesticide and the capture of potato bugs seemed tiresome and boring after a while, my least favorite chore would prove to be a wealth of Truth-drenched wisdom that would prove vitally useful in my later years. That chore? Weeding the garden!

Nearly every day of each week, my mother would assign me a particular row or sets of rows of vegetables to weed in the garden. Using the hoe I had been assigned, I would make my way up and down each row of that garden, chopping the tops off the green shoots of weeds that had somehow made their way into the row. It was easy to see the weeds that grew between the corn rows but difficult to see the weeds that grew between the bushy stalks of the ever-expanding green beans. I quickly came to realize that I could skip some of the weeds in the rows of green beans since my work—or lack thereof—would be obscured!

This worked well for me until a week or two had passed and my mother's inspection called my weeding skills into question. Pulling back the bushy heads of the green bean plants, she showed me where the weeds that I thought had been hidden so well had almost overgrown and overtaken the plants we were depending on for food. After this, she took me to the rows of corn I thought I had done a great job on but were being overtaken by weeds as well.

"I thought you told me you had weeded these rows of corn and that you had weeded the rows of green beans!"

My feeble response: "But, Mom, I did!"

Firmly, she took me back to the rows of green beans and had me kneel down and pull back the leaves of the bushy green bean plants. "Son, weeds grow where you cannot necessarily see. Just because you can't see them does not mean they aren't there. And those weeds among the corn? Just because you use a hoe and chop them down does not mean they are not still there. You never kill a weed until you get to the root. You can chop off the top of the weed all day long and never get rid of it. That means you're going to have to expose the weeds among the green beans and you're going to need to pull them up by hand, roots and all. Same with the corn. And don't just leave the weed plants nearby. Place them in the burn pile otherwise they will take root wherever you throw them. You must dispose of them properly."

As with weeds in a garden, we can allow wrong thinking to take root in our minds, or we can chop at them with good intentions; or, we can get to the root of those wrong thoughts and rid them from the garden of our mind once and for all. Which sounds like the better option to you? Of course you opted for the truth, right? Yet, you still find yourself a bit bewildered as to exactly how to do that. First things first. Just what is the truth? Until we settle that issue, we might as well be chopping off the tops of the weeds—or worse still, pretending they can't be seen.

3

POINT OF VIEW

How do you view the world around you? How does this worldview define who you are?

When contemplating the renewing of one's mind—the changing of the way one thinks—one must have a clear and sturdy foundation from which to operate, a solid rock that cannot be shaken when it seems the entire world around you is falling to pieces. If we have a firm foundation from which to launch our thought life, we can walk in peace in the midst of a storm. We can walk in health while our body is wracked with pain. We can walk in joy in the very throes of sorrow. We can think clearly when the world has clearly lost its mind!

When faced with the dilemma of what to believe about one's self, one must determine the foundation from which they currently operate. To simplify what I am speaking of, we must understand that every human thinks according to a certain worldview. From my own experience of walking out the journey of renewing one's mind, I have come to the personal conclusion that there are three worldviews available to every man, woman, and child. A worldview is how we as humans view reality. Like the skeleton from which grows the flesh of our existence, how we view the world around us is our reference point for ideas and attitudes. This point of view shapes how we explain our very existence and define our purpose in life. Bottom line, our worldview is our comprehensive and over-arching system of beliefs.

One worldview that is as old as sin is the man-centric worldview. Some call it humanism. If man is the utmost and highest, then every aspect of life must be viewed from that perspective. This kind of thinking leads to mankind thinking there is none higher than mankind. Man-centric thinking can lead to mass belief in wrong thinking. Ask Germany what they think of Hitler. Ask North Korea what they think of Kim Jong-un. I operated from this point of view for much of my youth, following whatever whim of human wisdom and new thinking brought into my life. This only led to disappointment and starving for the next idea that I could pin my hopes to.

Another major problem with man-centric thinking is that every man, at some point, fails. Every man dies. Even the greatest thinkers have all died. Einstein. Edison. Where is the hope in that? What happens when humanism comes up with a new point of view to take the place of the last one? Where is the stability in that? To place one's hope in a humanistic way of thinking is like building a house of straw and hoping it will protect you from fire. One spark is all it takes to cause that house to disintegrate. That is not a foundation from which I wanted my life built. I needed something more secure and stable.

Another worldview is the God-centric or Christ-centered worldview. If I believe God made all that I see and made all that I am, my way of thinking about reality and about myself takes on a whole new dimension. From that point of view, I come to realize that I have believed many lies about myself and about the world around me. Of course, this begs the question, *Where do those lies come from?* If I operate from a God-centric worldview, I take God's Word—the Bible—as the Truth from which to operate and from which to build my identity. That Word tells me there is a deceiver, the liar, Satan. He is vilely opposed to God and desires to destroy God's greatest creation: mankind. He does that through deception. This, of course, means the main battleground of my life is my mind. If we operate from the darkness of Satan's lies, we walk apart from the God Who created us for fellowship with Himself. My victory over same sex attraction, over the lies of the enemy in general, has come from changing the way I think about the world around me. I now strive to see life from God's point of view.

Yet one more worldview in even more sinister than the humanistic worldview; this worldview I call the mixed worldview. From my experience, there have been times when I tried to operate from a mixture of the man-centric and God-centric points of view. Like straddling a fence, this war of two opposing points of view leads to much pain and heartache. The tendency when mixing worldviews is to blame God when things fall apart. One cannot serve two masters. A two-headed beast is called a monster for a reason! A monster demands to be fed. A monster operates from a self-centered point of view. A monster hurts rather than heals. A monster leads one to fear rather than to trust. A monster cannot ever be satisfied. Why serve a monster? Why operate from such a shaky and shady foundation?

When deciding upon how to view the world, one must decide how the world came into existence in the first place. Either a big bang made it happen or God spoke it into existence. Those are our choices, according to the two worldviews we just talked about. I find it rather hypocritical for those who operate from a humanistic worldview to have no problem with the theory—the faith—that says we were planted here on Earth by some alien race, yet have no faith to believe God could have spoken us into existence. Before you get to the place of renewing your mind and to the place of the hope for change, you must decide how you will view the world. Do you want something tangible and real or do you want a counterfeit? Thinking from God's perspective leads to utter freedom and utter reality. Man-centric thinking leads to nothingness.

When I was a teenager, I loved listening to pop music. We were a hardworking farm family, but we had very little extra cash for things as frivolous as the latest record. Many were the hours I spent listening to the radio and longing to have an LP of my own so I could play my favorite songs over and over again and again without the frustration I found in hoping the radio station would play those songs. Blessed was the day I heard a TV commercial touting a collection of the top songs of that year containing all the top songs of the day!

After several weeks of saving my hard-earned cash from chores I had done on the farm, I sent away for that album and then waited. Every day, I went to the mailbox in the hope of finding that record. Finally, the day came when the postman came to the door of our farmhouse and handed me a large square cardboard packet that would not fit in the mailbox! My record! I rushed right up the stairs to the attic bedroom I shared with my three little brothers and placed it on the turntable. With ecstasy and exhilaration I gently placed the needle on the first song and went into a state of nirvana as the notes of the very familiar instrumental intro began to waft through the room. And then, the voice...

As I listened, something did not seem right. The singer sounded similar to the voice I had become so familiar with from the radio...but it was *off*. I thought this was supposed to be Mick Jagger! As I went to the next song expecting to hear Stevie Wonder, I was again disappointed and mystified at the voice that sounded mostly *like* Stevie's very familiar voice...but without the extra little vocal flourishes I had come to expect from him. Each song left me with the same thought: They sounded similar but were obviously not the original singers of the songs I loved. Upon closer inspection of the album liner notes, I discovered the small print: "Each song sung by a sound-alike artist." These were fakes! I felt used and humiliated! I felt, frankly, stupid and gullible and decided I would never buy a sound-alike recording again. Only the real thing for me! Deciding upon your worldview is much the same. You can settle for the fake—or counterfeit—or you can seek the real thing.

I find it very interesting that when a government agent is being taught how to discern real US currency from counterfeit, he or she is never shown the counterfeit. They get to know the real money so well that when the counterfeit crosses their path, it is easily recognized as the fake it is. Deciding how you will view the world will be derived from that which you seek. If you seek to view the world from a humanistic point of view, you will one day find yourself let down by the weakness of such a perspective. May I challenge you to seek God through a relationship with Jesus Christ as the better—the real—perspective from which to operate?

What is your worldview? What would you have to lose by considering viewing the world from the point of view of the Maker of that world? Is it man-central or God/Christ-central? Another way to put it,

- Is your hope in government or government programs? How is that working out for you?

- Is your hope in another person? Anyone let you down lately? Just wait. They will.

- Is your hope in financial success? What happens when you lose everything you hold dear because your focus was solely on finding your reality in financial success? What happens if you lose it all?

- Is your hope in fame? Do you really think being famous will add one iota of hope to your existence? What happens when you're not the cool kid anymore?

- Is your hope in what others think of you? What happens when you fail? What happens when they turn on you? What happens when you face loneliness? Does the fear of what people think of you determine how you view yourself? Does it determine your choices in life? Is that a good way to live?

- Is your hope in God? You need to decide before any true change is even possible.

"No one can serve two masters; for either he will hate the one and love the other, or he will be devoted to one and despise the other. You cannot serve God and wealth." —Jesus (Matthew 6:24)

I know your deeds, that you are neither cold nor hot; I wish that you were cold or hot. So because you are lukewarm, and neither hot nor cold, I will spit you out of My mouth. (Revelation 3:15-16)

4

FIRST THINGS FIRST

I f you have determined how you are going to view the world by choosing to see it through the lens of God's point of view, there is another point of decision you must come to before you proceed. You must become like a child. A child trusts his or her parent to catch them when they leap for their arms. That is how we must trust God: by becoming like children. To do that, you must be born again.

> *"Truly I say to you, whoever does not receive the kingdom of God like a child will not enter it at all." —Jesus (Luke 18:17)*

> *Jesus answered and said to him, "Truly, truly, I say to you, unless one is born again he cannot see the kingdom of God." (John 3:3)*

Because of my story of freedom from same-sex attraction due to my relationship with God through faith in Jesus Christ, I have many people tell me they long to know God intimately, long to be forgiven, long to be healed of past wounds, long to be free from whatever, long to be made brand new. For too long I believe the church has made knowing God more about jumping through religious hoops than about connecting people to a real and present God who desires an intimate relationship with them. Knowing God intimately in a real-life relationship is as simple as a step of faith.

Why do we need God? Simple: We were created for fellowship with Him; but something about God's love led Him to never force us to love Him. He gave us a choice in the matter. And what did we do with that choice? Turned from God and gave in to sin. One sin was all it took to separate you and I from relationship with a holy God. One sin separates us from holy God. Make no mistakes. God is a God of love. He does not send a man to hell. A man's sin sends him to hell. Every man, every woman, every single child, has sinned. This can't be helped because we are born into a sinful world.

For all have sinned, and come short of the glory of God. (Romans 3:23 NKJV)

Does it seem that the world just keeps growing darker and darker and that people aren't as good as you would have hoped? Does your life seem like you are simply going from one difficult circumstance to another? Have you ever wondered why things are never perfect? Why is there war? Why is there poverty? Why does the world seem to be riddled with so much pain? Sin sees to it that death comes. God intended us to live, but sin ushered death into the world.

For the wages of sin [is] death; but the gift of God [is] eternal life through Jesus Christ our Lord. (Romans 6:23 NKJV)

So what are we to do to remedy our sin separation from God?

Jesus answered..., "Most assuredly, I say to you, unless one is born again, he cannot see the kingdom of God." (John 3:3 NKJV)

What does it mean to be born again? What does it mean to be saved from our sin? We were created by God for fellowship with Him. Sin came into the world by our own choosing and death is the result. Since God is perfect and cannot fellowship with sin, a way had to be made to restore us to God. That way? Jesus Christ.

Jesus was perfect. In His perfection He was tempted in every manner just as we are, yet He never sinned. This made Him the perfect candidate to save us from our sin. How did that happen? Simple. Jesus Christ took your sin and my sin upon Himself. He suffered the punishment for that sin by being put to death on the cross. He died with our sin upon Him and our sin was buried with Him.

But good news! Jesus did not stay dead! He rose to life and left sin in the grave and conquered death for us! If we place our faith in Him, he will give us a brand new identity. How do we do that?

> ...*if you confess with your mouth the Lord Jesus and believe in your heart that God has raised Him from the dead, you will be saved. For with the heart one believes unto righteousness, and with the mouth confession is made unto salvation. (Romans 10:9-10 NKJV)*

Simply put, confess that Jesus Christ is Lord (which means He is Master of all life and Lord over your own life) and then believe—a step of faith—that God has raised Him from the dead, and you will be saved. You will be born again!

> ...*if anyone is in Christ, he is a new creation; old things have passed away; behold, all things have become new. (2 Corinthians 5:17 NKJV)*

When I got tired of being homosexual, I decided I had played god with my own life long enough. I gave up to the real and true God. I realized Jesus Christ took my homosexuality upon Himself. I realized that the blood Jesus gave up for me paid the debt of sin I could not pay. I realized that the old "me" was crucified with Christ and buried with Him. I realized that Jesus had risen and was calling me to new life in Him. I walked out of my old life and have been pursuing my new one ever since. I became someone brand new—a new creation!

Did the temptations stop right away? No. But temptations no longer defined me. Temptation gives me the opportunity to become intimate and transparent and honest with Christ through faith. I no longer had to perform for anyone's love or approval. I suddenly found myself completely accepted by Him. All I ever have to do is to believe and receive His love for me in any situation. Jesus understands. Sin will always be in the world until Jesus returns. But Jesus understands.

> ...*we do not have a high priest [Jesus] who is unable to sympathize with our weaknesses, but we have one who has been tempted in every*

way, just as we are—yet was without sin. Let us then approach the throne of grace with confidence, so that we may receive mercy and find grace to help us in our time of need. (Hebrews 4:15-16 NIV)

Would you like to be saved? To be born again? Are you tired of being so alone against the temptations of life? Would you like to have a Faithful Friend who walks through each and every day—each and every trial—with you? Then pray (prayer is simply talking with God just as you would talk with a person you could see) this simple prayer in faith:

"Lord Jesus. I have sinned, and I need a Savior. I confess out loud, here and now, that You are Lord. I believe, by placing my faith in You, that God has raised You from the dead. Save me, Lord."

If you prayed that prayer, it's a "done deal." You are signed, sealed, and delivered, His! Now what do you do? Go to His Word and learn more about His ways. Find other believers of Jesus and build relationships with them. Build a deep and ever-growing relationship with Jesus by including Him in every aspect of your life. He can handle your junk... your rants and ravings. He is kind and patient and will never betray you. Trust Him to teach you how to hear His voice.

God saved you by his special favor when you believed. And you can't take credit for this; it is a gift from God. Salvation is not a reward for the good things we have done, so none of us can boast about it. For we are God's masterpiece. He has created us anew in Christ Jesus, so that we can do the good things he planned for us long ago. (Ephesians 2:8-10 NLT)

I have a friend who summed up what I am trying to say in a very concise way. One day as she talked with her gay hair dresser, they began talking about identity. Concerned that he may be walking in an identity opposed to the will of God, the hair dresser simply said, "I'm not sure I want to be gay, but that's how I feel."

My friend responded with this question: "If you could go back to your mother's womb and you could choose to be either gay or straight, what would you choose?"

His reply? "I would choose to be straight."

In wisdom, she said, "In a sense, you can do that very thing. You can choose to be born again into a new identity in Christ."

Being born again—becoming a new creation in Christ—is a simple step of faith. If you just took that step of faith, you are someone you were not before. All the old things have, by faith, passed away. You no longer have to be defined by your past. You do not even have to worry about changing your past. It cannot be done anyway! But the great news of a God-centric point of view is that God is able to take even our failures and make something beautiful of them. By faith, new things have come. A brand new identity that transcends the way you may feel about yourself. A brand new identity full of untapped possibilities in this life. This is a new day and a new dawn of self-discovery for you. This is going to be the most incredible journey!

Being born again will drastically and dramatically alter the way you think about reality and about yourself. It will dramatically change the way you view God as well. In fact, everything is going to change. The more your thoughts change, the more your feelings will change. The more your thoughts change, the more your attitudes and behaviors will follow suit. I urge you to never get too far away from that childlike faith that led you to this moment. An entire new realm and kingdom are now open to you as you learn to pursue a relationship with your Maker and discover who He says you are. Are you ready?

Now go and simply be his child!

5

HOW DO YOU FEEL?

For as he thinks within himself, so he is.
(Proverbs 23:7)

W ho made us emotional beings? Who made us with the ability to feel? Why do we feel? If we have a man-centric worldview, our emotions are the feelings we happen to be born with. In other words, they are part of what defines us as humans. What we have is what we get. This is just the way we are wired. We live in a world and a culture in which how a person feels defines who we are. As of this writing, there are currently fifty-eight different gender identities to choose from.[2]

According to Miley Cyrus, she is gender fluid based on her feelings. She is quoted as saying, "It's literally just how I feel."[3] Gender fluidity means a person's gender can fluctuate depending upon how they feel alone, regardless of their chromosome count! I find it interesting that a person's feelings about themselves can change even in a man-centric

---

2. Russell Goldman, "Here's a List of 58 Gender Options for Facebook Users," (February, 2014). http://abcnews.go.com/blogs/headlines/2014/02/heres-a-list-of-58-gender-options-for-facebook-users/.

3. Colin Stutz, "Miley Cyrus Says She's Gender Fluid: 'It Has Nothing to Do with Any Parts of Me,'" (June, 2015). http://www.billboard.com/articles/columns/pop-shop/6598191/miley-cyrus-gender-fluid-nothing-to-do-with-any-parts.

society. That fact alone should tell us something—namely that changing the way one feels is completely possible!

When I was a boy, I felt so opposite of what I thought a boy should feel like that I would not even allow myself to put my hands in my pockets—because that's what real boys do—and I just simply did not feel like a boy! The way we think affects the way we feel. The way we feel affects our attitudes and our behaviors. Wrong thinking, when left unchecked, results in bad habits. My warped way of thinking led me to all manners of unhealthy behavior: promiscuity, suicidal tendencies, angry outbursts, and utter self-focus.

A great example of what I am talking about grew out of my wrong thinking about my anger. Because I was such an artistic, touchy feely, and outside-of-the-normal-way-of-thinking kind of a guy, I would have moments of anger in which I lost control. I did not understand myself, my gifts, or my emotional tendencies, nor did I understand what it meant to be introverted. My parents did not understand me either. This lack of understanding—and wrong thinking on my part—led to such frustration that I would blow up in anger if one of my brothers crossed me in some innocent way, or if I did not win at a competition when playing with my cousins, or when my parents would ask me to do something I thought was beneath me to do.

On more than one such occasion, my mom would respond to my anger—often while disciplining me—with, "You come by your anger naturally. Your great-grandparents were angry people. This is just the way you are." Even though I always felt remorse after realizing that my anger had just hurt whomever I was unleashing my wrath upon, the words I believed about myself always assuaged the guilt to some degree. If this was just the way I was, then people will just have to get over it when I vomit out my vitriol. The only problem was that no one wants to be around an angry person! The way we think affects the way we feel. The way we feel affects how we respond to life and reality. The way we respond to others will also have an affect upon them. Wrong thinking leads us to self-wounding, and hurt people hurt people.

One of the first things the Lord began to deal with me about after He changed my identity was to face my anger. He simply asked me by way of my thoughts, in that silent voice I have come to understand as the voice of God to me, "Who told you you were an angry man?"

My response? "My family."

Without missing a beat, my Father God asked me, "Who made you, son?"

"You did, Lord."

"Then be the man of peace I say you are. That old way of thinking about yourself was never from Me, son. Let us rip that old way of thinking away from your mind. See what's exposed there? That is the heart of peace I planted in you when you were first born again. Just be that."

In that moment, everything about the way I thought about myself took yet another amazing turn toward freedom and made me re-evaluate everything I believed about myself and about who God says He is. It led me to ask these questions: Does God feel anything? Is He an emotional God?

> *When Jesus went ashore, He saw a large crowd, and He felt compassion for them because they were like sheep without a shepherd; and He began to teach them many things. (Mark 6:34)*

Jesus and the Father are One. Jesus felt compassion. God feels compassion. Jesus once burst into anger at the way people were using the house of God in an unholy manner. God can feel anger; He can feel peace; He can weep with sorrow; He can feel joy! He is the One who made our emotions. So why would He make us emotional beings?

Though not exhaustive by any means, I believe God made us emotional beings for several reasons. Emotions help us sense God and feel His presence. During some of my most depraved moments, I have felt God's presence. What I have come to realize in looking back at such moments is that God was actually presenting me with His thoughts, and the feeling of His presence with me was triggered by some Truth He was presenting me—like the many moments I contemplated suicide and felt that God was there asking me to reconsider. In looking back, I know now that He was there simply saying, "I am here, son…and I love you."

Another purpose of emotions is to help us pinpoint pain and aids in the dealing with and healing of that pain. Let's say we have a pain in our side and it does not subside after several days, only increases in intensity. What do we do? We head for the doctor. The first thing the doctor says is something like, "Show me where it hurts." Our response is to show him and allow him to do the work necessary to bring about our healing. The only drawback would be if we were to respond to the doctor with, "What will people think of me if I show you?" What if we walked out of that encounter and the pain grew into death? That would be foolish, would it not? Yet that is exactly what we do with our feelings and our wrong thoughts when faced with honesty before God. Why is that? Could it be because of our wrong worldview? Unless we view God as our Maker, we will never have our emotional needs met in a lasting way by an imperfect world.

Emotions are like rivers of the soul that transport us to the deep places of God's presence. Feelings of sorrow lead me to cry out to God for comfort. Feelings of depravity lead me to seek Him for cleansing. Feelings of need lead me to cry out to Him for provision. Feelings of emotional wounding cause me to cry out to Him for healing. Even when I feel nothing—numbness—such non-feeling causes me to cry out to Him for emotional wholeness and filling. And when I am honest about those feelings, they were always attached to some thought I have had that has led me to that feeling. Feelings are not bad. They are necessary to help us function as human beings in need of a holy God. Feelings help us discern our God in ways that transcend what our eyes can see. Our goal, as new creations, should be to feel what our Father feels. In order to do that, we must think as He thinks! And I have wonderful news! As a new creation, you have been given the mind of Christ! You can think His thoughts. And to think like Christ is to have one's mind set free to operate in the way it was intended all along!

For WHO HAS KNOWN THE MIND OF THE LORD, THAT HE WILL INSTRUCT HIM? But we have the mind of Christ. (1 Corinthians 2:16)

Should feelings define a person—give them their identity? Who wants to be defined by their feelings? I feel anger at times, but I do not want to be identified as an angry man. I want to be identified as a new creation who is slow to anger. Who wants to be defined by their appetites? I want my appetites to be used for the King and for the kingdom of God!

Would you be willing to explore the possibility that your self-thought processes may have been compromised by wrong-thinking or by a wrong perception of self? To do so will lead you to a journey of transformation and the renewing of your mind…a renewal of the way you think.

When I first walked out of my homosexual past, I was told I would be back by my still-gay friends. I was told I was faking my way through life to sell music and make a living in the Christian music world. And my favorite? I was told I had been brainwashed. And, you know what? To that one I had to agree. As I began to put off the lies that were opposed to God's design for me as a man, my thought-life was being washed by the Truth of God's complete design for my masculine identity!

> *Therefore I urge you, brethren, by the mercies of God, to present your bodies a living and holy sacrifice, acceptable to God, which is your spiritual service of worship. And do not be conformed to this world, but be transformed by the renewing of your mind, so that you may prove what the will of God is, that which is good and acceptable and perfect. (Romans 12:1-2)*

How many other feelings do you have that you know to be wrong but are hard to shake? Habits can be broken as we change the way we think about our identity from God's point of view. Hunger for food can become hunger for God's Word. Craving for drugs to alter the way we feel and to cope with life can become craving for God's Truth and presence to bathe us in His love and acceptance. Lust for the same sex can be seen as the counterfeit it is as we hunger after God's Truth for His design and purpose for our sexuality.

If feelings are deeply ingrained, does that mean they're God given? As we have already discussed, Satan is the liar and deceiver opposed to God's will and way. Since his only power over us is in the lies he plants in our minds, we know where to attack him and how to push him back. It is by the Word of God. A God-centric worldview leads to new thinking and new thinking leads to self-control. Self-control leads to victory over stinkin' thinkin'.

What does God require of us when our deep feelings take us one way and His will takes us another? We need but look to Jesus who did not feel like going to the cross, yet He chose to go against His feelings. Those feelings were a means of connecting to God and operating in God's reality…which led to the whole world being given the opportunity to be saved from sin. To be saved from stinkin' thinkin'.

Are you ready to be free?

6

CORE IDENTITY

As I was growing up, it never dawned on me to think about my core identity—the deepest part of me that defines who I am. When puberty hit and my sexual identity became more solidified toward attraction to those of the same sex, I began to question a bit. Why was I attracted to other males? How do I fix this? It led me to beg God to change me. When nothing changed, I became disillusioned in my faith, concluding this was simply the way God made me. But the older I became, the less happy I was in a homosexual identity. This lack of happiness led me to question on a deeper level. Is this all there is?

As I became involved with other men who believed they were homosexual, I became more confused. I was constantly told that this was just the way God made me. I was constantly encouraged that I had no choice in the matter at all. Mulling such thoughts over in my mind, I could never quite reconcile these simple answers with the way I felt. This led me to the constant questioning of my homosexuality. Was this truly my nature or was there more to the story? The more I questioned my homosexual identity, the more desperate those questions became. Desperation led me to wonder whether or not I might just have a choice in the matter after all.

I will not detail my story here. If you want to know more about how I came to the place of belief I now walk, read my autobiography, *Sing Over Me*. Suffice it to say, I came ultimately to the conclusion that I did *not* have a choice as to what would tempt me (same sex attraction), but I always had the choice as to how I would respond to it. After coming to faith in Christ, my worldview became Christ-centered. This new focus became the bedrock from which I launched the journey of renewing my mind, completely altering the way I would think from that point on!

Where is core identity found? In our body? In our genitals? In our feelings? In our heart? In our mind? Is identity found in our culture—the way we were raised? Is it found in our ethnicity or our nationality? Is it found in our personality type or in our profession? Is it to be found in the way others perceive us? Does our sexuality define us? How about our religion? How about our language? Are we defined by our genetic code? Are we defined by our convictions or causes (pacifist, environmentalist, Black Lives Matter, conservative, liberal, etc.)? Are we defined by our looks? Some would say it is a combination of all these things that make us who we are. The scientific community would sum it up like this: identity is the qualities, beliefs, personality, looks, and/or expressions that make a person who they are. Identity is conscious awareness.

But let's think logically about where all these various defining things emanate from. Do they not all begin and end with the way we think? Could it be our identity begins and ends with the mind? Could it be that in order to alter our undesired habits and ways of thinking about ourselves we need but change the way we think? I know this is easier said than done, but isn't our well-being worth the work required to obtain it? Identity is conscious awareness as received in our thoughts. It is our human mind!

We are constantly thinking about ourselves. How does that person view me? What do I want to eat? What shall I wear today? Do I like hanging around that person? How will spending time with them benefit my life? Will this job pay enough to finance my vision for my life? Will that vaccination hurt me? How will this election affect me? Even in our sleep we never stop talking to ourselves. Never. The way we think about ourselves has a direct affect upon the way we live our life. The way we think affects our view of reality. My reality was forever altered the day I decided to live and think about myself according to the way my Maker designed me. Of course, this flew directly in the face of the way I felt. The best decision I ever made was to stop defining myself by the way I felt and start living according to the Truth as defined by God and His Word. This began the most incredible journey of my life!

What does it mean to know something in one's heart? This can be confusing, yet we hear such questions all the time. How many times have you heard a question such as, How do I get that knowledge from my head to my heart? And that is a perfectly good question, especially when we hear of scientific studies proving that the heart does indeed have brain-like cells, giving it the ability to think independently of the brain![4] Simply put, science is coming to the place of thinking that the *thoughts* produced by the heart act as a communication between the various cells and organs of the body, acting as a sort of synchronizing signal for the entire body! The way I think about this news is that the mind defines us in our core and the heart carries this information to the rest of our body!

While this is fascinating to know, for our intents and purposes I will conclude that identity begins and ends with the way we think about ourselves in our mind. What does it mean to know something in one's mind? Could it be said that one is defined by what one thinks of him/herself? Could it be that, ultimately, we should define ourselves according to the way our Maker designed us? If we have as our thought-foundation a Christ-centric worldview, then we must come to this conclusion found in God's Word:

For as he thinks within himself, so he is. (Proverbs 23:7)

In order to renew one's mind, one must operate from some point of view. My freedom and new identity came from allowing God to define me—came from seeking to know His, the Maker's, point of view concerning Dennis Jernigan. The following are some of the questions

---

4. Rollin McCraty, Raymond Trevor Bradley, Dana Tomasino, "The Heart Has its Own 'Brain' and Consciousness," (January, 2015). http://in5d.com/the-heart-has-its-own-brain-and-consciousness/.

He confronted me with accompanied by the answers He showed me according to His Word:

1. Why did God make man and woman?

   From my own experience with and study of God's Word, I believe there is a two-fold reason God made man and woman. This is what the Word of God says:

   Be fruitful and multiply… (Genesis 35:11)

   Husbands, love your wives, just as Christ also loved the church and gave Himself up for her… (Ephesians 5:25)

   My conclusion after reading the Word and viewing my life from God's point of view? Man and woman were created by God and commanded to make babies! If He created me to be a man, it was for the purpose of making more people! That cannot be accomplished according to God's design by having sex with another man. Cannot be done. God desired more of us because He created us for fellowship with Him. The sin of mankind was the problem. Where does sin derive from? Man thinking it's all about him! Sin comes from stinkin' thinin'!

2. What is the primary purpose of sex?

   God made sex for the purpose of procreation. He made it pleasurable so we would want to experience it. Pure and simple, without sex there would be no more humans. There is nothing wrong with pleasure as long as it is derived within the confines of God's ultimate design. After settling that God was God and that His design would define me, the questions became even more specific.

3. Did God give you a penis and testicles or did He give you a vagina and ovaries?

   Having a penis and testicles defined me as being physically male. Being physically male made me wonder why I did not have feelings of attraction to the opposite sex. Concluding that

I had been lied to was the first step in putting off the lies about the way I felt—or did not feel! Although I initially did not feel attracted to women, I did have the desire for a family. This led me to the conclusion that if that desire was there, then it must be part of my design to feel attracted to a woman. From that conclusion, I came to the place of realizing that my feelings of attraction to other men was simply as a result of wrong thinking. The reality became simple to me at that point. Whenever I felt attraction to another man, I renounced it as a result of wrong thinking and replaced that wrong thinking with simple thoughts like, *God made me physically a man; therefore he made me to think like a man. I want to see a woman in the way God designed me to see her. Father God, please replace the wrong thoughts with right thoughts and replace the wrong feelings with right feelings.*

The more I changed the way I thought, the more my true needs and desires were met. My despair over my feelings was slowly but surely being replaced with right feelings due to the way I was now thinking! God's Word says in Psalm 37:4,

Delight yourself in the LORD; And He will give you the desires of your heart.

The more I sought relationship with Him through the ways I thought about Him and His Word and how it applied to my life, the more my feelings changed. Even my sexual attractions toward men began to be replaced by attractions to women. So much mental healing had taken place in my life from 1981 to 1983 that I was able to realize a dream I never thought possible due to my homosexual feelings. I was able to marry Melinda, and as of this writing, I have been married for over thirty-three years, have nine awesome children, and nine incredible grandchildren...so far!

The changing of the way I thought about myself actually began much more simplistically than that. To renew the way I thought about myself as a man, I asked the Lord to reveal any wrong thinking I had about myself. In order to do this, I realized that I had been listening to the liar for far too long in my existence. But how would I cut off the voice of the liar? I went on what would become a twelve year fast from all the other voices of influence that were not God centered. From 1981 until 1993, I did not listen to pop/secular music. I did not watch TV. I listened to only voices that built me up according to God's design for my life. In the process, I learned to discern the voice and will of God more clearly.

As I silenced the other voices, I gave God the freedom to speak to me in any form He chose for me. His Word became alive to me. From reading God's Word, I discovered how loving and *for me* He was! I discovered He was never disgusted with me but was disgusted with my sin. I discovered that I no longer had to perform for His love and acceptance. It had always been my choice to receive or reject! That Truth alone changed everything! Gone were the days of trying to prove my worth by my performance. This meant I performed *because* He loved me rather than *so* He would love me!

The more I discovered about Who He said He was, the more I discovered who He designed me to be. He is holy. I am set apart for His purposes in this life. He is righteous. I am to walk righteously. He is peace. He has planted a heart of peace in me and set my mind at peace. He is Healer. I am here to be an agent of His healing power. He is Provider. I am here to be an agent of His provision. He is Shepherd. I am here to guide others to Him. He is always there. I am never alone. He is victorious over sin. I am no longer a victim of my own sin but am victor over it because of Him!

Even though my circumstances did not change, the way I viewed them did! I could choose to think what thoughts I wanted to think. That was incredible news and incredibly freeing. Rather than overthinking everything about myself from a man-centric point of view, I could simplify my thought processes to such a degree that freedom was the result simply by allowing the Word and intended design of God for me as the filter through which I viewed reality.

So much healing has come to my mind to this point that it is difficult for me to believe I ever thought I was gay in the first place. Let that sink in. Freedom comes from the way we choose to think about ourselves. Will you allow stinkin' thinkin' to define you? Will you let past failure define you? Will you allow other people to define you? Will you allow feelings to define you? Will you allow temptation to define you? Will you allow bad habits to define you?

If there is something that you habitually think about yourself that you do not desire, could it be said you are allowing that thought to define you? Why put up with that way of thinking? Does your desire for drugs define you or do they reveal a deeper need for thinking about your circumstances in a new way? Will you be content with being a victim of your own stinkin' thinkin' or will you choose to seek victory over that way of thinking? The choice really is yours.

One of the best things I ever did to facilitate right thinking about myself as a man was to enlist the help of others in my life. I felt guilty about the failures of my life, especially in regard to my sexual failure. I felt so much shame that I believed the lie that I was not worthy of someone else's time or effort or love. Guilt is the awareness that I did something wrong. Shame is the belief that I am something wrong. We kick shame to the curb by getting to the Truth of God's Word and the reality of His design for us as new creations. When I dealt with my shame in honesty and came to the mental conclusion that Jesus Christ had born all my shame on the cross, I took the first step toward Truth and freedom: I got honest with myself. I got honest with God. I got honest with others.

One of my choices was to surround myself with people who would help me walk in the Truth of my God-designed identity. To this day, I practice this in my life. My wife and my children have the freedom to remind me who and Whose I am. One of my personal rules is that Dennis Jernigan does not get to call himself something his Father does not call him. I cannot even get away with little slip-ups like saying to myself, "Stupid idiot" when I do something boneheaded! My wife and my children automatically say to me, "Is that who you really are?" or, "Is that who God says you are?" And I love it because I know they absolutely love me and want nothing but what is best for me. Stinkin' thinkin' is recognized in the moment. I put it off and replace it with the Truth...and move on down the road to my whole identity in Christ!

No longer do I define myself as ex-gay. No longer do I define myself as a recovering or formal homosexual. No longer do I define myself. My Father has that place in my life, and He uses other people to help me. I am what and who His Word says I am. And so are you.

Would you be willing to consider seeing yourself from a whole new point of view? If so, read on!

7

WHO FATHER GOD SAYS
WE ARE

I f we are new creations in Christ, we need to view our life from that
vantage point, rather than from any other point of view. This is both
freeing and humbling. When I think about who and Whose I am, I think
about my childhood and the way I was raised. I think about who my
father is and was. So much about me and the way I perceived my identity
was based on what I learned from him. Whether we like it or not, we are
heavily influenced by our parents—or lack thereof. Parents—especially
our fathers—have great power when it comes to bestowing identity upon
their children. That is simply a fact, again, whether we like it or not. If we
perceive our father to be proud of us, we tend to walk in confidence. If
we perceive him to be displeased with us, we tend to question everything
about ourselves. That was my story.

Everything changed when I replaced my man-centric worldview
with a God-centric worldview. Not only did I begin to view myself in
a whole new way, I also viewed my perceptions of my father and the
way he raised me in a whole new light. I stopped blaming my father for
my wrong choices. I stopped blaming him for the way I thought about
myself. How did I accomplish that? Certainly not on my own! It was
Father God and others who helped me put off the old ways of thinking

and replace them with the new way of thinking that brought me to the place of freedom I have come to enjoy.

Rather than identifying myself by the way I perceived how my earthly father saw me (which was skewed and perverted, to say the least!), I chose to view myself and think about myself from the vantage point of my heavenly Father. As I said previously, one of my personal rules to this day is that Dennis Jernigan does not get to call himself something his Father does not call him! But, again, just how did I get to the Father's point of view? I had to become like a child.

> *"Truly I say to you, whoever does not receive the kingdom of God like a child will not enter it at all." —Jesus (Luke 18:17)*

What is it about becoming a child that brings us to the place of entering the kingdom of God, of entering into the kingdom point of view, the kingdom way of thinking? Let's think about the qualities of a child. A child trusts. A child desires to know his or her father. A child pursues his father. A child wants to know her father. A child believes it when his or her father expresses joy over their existence. A child is ready for the father's embrace and finds joy in just being with him. A child jumps into thin air when they know their father is ready and willing and able to catch them! How did I get to know my Father? I asked Him to reveal to me who He says He is. In so doing, I believed knowing His nature would reveal mine. Jesus, when He was a boy, actively sought to know His heavenly Father, even risking alienation from his earthly parents. Once, He remained behind in the town synagogue when His parents headed for home. After searching high and low, they found Him with the church leaders and elders. The response of Jesus?

> *"Did you not know that I must be about My Father's business?" (Luke 2:49 NKJV)*

A major part of our Father's business is leading people to know Him. That is why He sent Jesus to Earth in the first place! So, let us begin there in the process of renewing our mind. Let's lay down all our pre-conceived notions about Who God is, and let us be open to having our misconceptions about His character sent packing. Knowing Who He says He is will help us determine who we were/are created to be!

A good name is to be more desired than great wealth,
Favor is better than silver and gold. (Proverbs 22:1)

In God's Word, He reveals much about Himself through the names He calls Himself. When I hear my own name, I hear the meaning of my name. Dennis means, "Follower of Dionysius, the Greek god of wine." When I was born again, one of the first things I was led to do was to redefine my name. Whenever I hear my name now, I hear, "Follower and worshiper of the one true God." That was and is a whole new way of seeing myself! That one mental rethinking moment was a major turning point in my self-thought life. Let's take a few of the names God calls Himself and then see how they apply to our own existence and identity, and then let's be open to a change of reality from darkness to light!

He calls Himself Jehovah Shammah in Ezekiel 48:35. It literally means, "The Lord is there." What does that mean? Regardless of where we find ourselves, regardless of how we feel, and regardless of our pain or circumstances, He is there *with us*! In fact, one of the names by which Jesus is known in Scripture is Immanuel, which means, "God with us" (Isaiah 7:14). We are never alone. When I was bound up in homosexual thought, I felt utterly alone for much of my life. But even in the midst of my feeling alone, the reality was that I was *never* alone. Not even one moment! As I began to look back on my life from that vantage point, I was able to see God as compassionate and always there pursuing me. I was able to find healing for the pain and wounds left by all those times I had felt alone by simply seeing my God's point of view! He loved me right where I was, even in the midst of depravity—but He loved me enough to not leave me there! That changed everything! I would never be alone again. Hallelujah!

He calls Himself Jehovah-Nissi, which means, "The Lord is my banner," or, "The Lord is my victory." In Exodus 15, Moses and Aaron led the children of Israel against the army of Amalek. The army of Israel was being pushed back, until Moses went to the top of a hill and lifted his arms. As he lifted his arms toward heaven, the army of Israel made headway. As his arms grew tired and fell to his side, they were again pushed back. In order to help hold his arms up, Aaron and a man named Hur helped hold the arms of Moses toward the sky, and Israel defeated the Amalekites! Moses named the place Jehovah-Nissi to remind the children of Israel that their God had brought about their victory.

What that means to my life is this: God is the same God to me that He was in the battle with Amalek! He has my back just as He had the back of Israel. Jesus was victorious over sin! I am born again in Him, therefore I have victory over sin. Before I believed this, I walked in constant defeat, believing my inability to overcome sin and failure was just who I was, I considered myself a complete failure. As I began to proclaim this Truth—Jesus is my Victory, therefore I am victorious— over my own mind, my feelings of defeat began to be replaced with feelings of triumph. I did not stop having moments of failure, but I decided to keep getting back up and heading for Jesus. I decided it was better to be a victor rather than to be a victim!

He calls Himself Jehovah Rohi in Psalm 23. It literally means, "The Lord my Shepherd." Whenever I thought of God before I knew Him, I thought of Him as a distant dictator or cosmic policeman. My view was that He waited for me in heaven to see if I would obey Him or not—and whenever He saw me fail, He would swoop down and bop me on the head and beat me back into line—into submission. This thought was reinforced by the way I treated a lamb I once owned. Her name was Abby. My job was to train Abby for the livestock show. My way of doing this? If she disobeyed, I struck her! I was so perplexed whenever I went for our daily training session only to find her cowering in the corner, obviously gripped by fear. I felt mortified! Terrible! My solution? I began to take her carrots and other goodies and began to treat her with kindness. After only a few days, the once-cowering lamb began to greet me at the gate and followed me wherever I led her.

When I was born again, I soon learned that Jesus is a good Shepherd! A good Shepherd never beats His sheep into submission, but leads them by example. As I applied this to my own life, I began to listen for the voice of Shepherd Jesus. He led me to clear fresh waters of understanding who I was called to be. He led me to fresh green lush pastures of His Word that began to transform the way I viewed reality... myself. He led me through the process of healing as He began to assess my wounds and began to apply the necessary balms of Truth to those same wounds. He led me to a feast of His presence in the very midst of my most dire circumstances.

Before I saw God as Good Shepherd, my view was pathetic. I saw myself as deserving of only sitting beneath the table of His presence and groveling for any crumbs that fell on my lowly head from somewhere above. All along He had been calling me to sit *at* the table and enjoy the feast of His presence—in *this* life! In *this* existence. That is how He sees me and how I began to see myself. A child of the Shepherd Who is the King, seated boldly at the table *with* Him! That was a life-altering point of view for sure.

He calls Himself Jehovah-Rapha, "The Lord that heals." In Exodus 15, God reveals His healing nature to the children of Israel who had just come out of slavery in Egypt. In spite of all the miracles God performed to get them out of bondage, they still longed for the security of those old chains—and He still chose to heal them of all the diseases that afflicted the Egyptians. How often do we feel that same way? At least in our old way of thinking we knew our limits. How sad is that way of thinking? And make no bones about it, it is a way of thinking! The Israelites had been enslaved to the Egyptians for four hundred years. That's a lot of time to build up the thought process that says, *This is just the way it is and this is just the way it will be.* While that may give you a measure of peace, it does not give you victory. This is a sickness—a wrong way of thinking—that can only be healed by changing the way one thinks.

If one does not believe they are sick, then one does not seek the Healer. My mental and spiritual healing began to be realized the day I chose to agree with God that I was sick in the way I thought about Him and about myself. I chose to put off the lies He revealed to me and then actively chose to put on the Truth according to His Word. It had taken me twenty-two years to build up the wall of lies I had believed. He encouraged me with the understanding that it may take time to tear down that wall and rebuild it with the Truth. Some lies have come down instantly while others have been a process. Some Truths have been grasped quickly while others have taken time to take root in my mind. Healing has come as I have chosen to trust my Healer rather than the wisdom of man.

In Jeremiah 23:6, God reveals Himself as Jehovah Tsidkenu, "The Lord Our Righteousness." This is actually a prophecy about the coming of the Savior, Jesus Christ. In 1 Corinthians we find this Truth:

> *But by His doing you are in Christ Jesus, who became to us wisdom from God, and righteousness and sanctification, and redemption. (1 Corinthians 1:30)*

When I was bound up in stinkin' thinkin', I felt (there's that word again) that my only recourse to my constant failure was to perform my way through life—to gain God's approval and acceptance and earn His love. That is how I *felt* about the people in my life as well. The feeling should have given me the clue to the Truth. Everything changed the day it dawned on me that there was absolutely no way to ever earn God's acceptance, approval, or love other than the free gift of simple faith in Jesus Christ. In the most simple terms I can convey this Truth: Jesus Christ exchanged His life for mine on the cross.

> *He [God] made Him who knew no sin to be sin on our behalf, so that we might become the righteousness of God in Him. (2 Corinthians 5:21)*

In other words, when He exchanged His life for mine, and I exchanged my way of thinking/life for His, I effectively became righteous in the sight of God. How could that not rock my world and drastically alter the way I thought about myself? This newfound way of thinking made me want to turn from my sin more than ever and to seek the righteous Savior Who set my thoughts spinning in the right direction.

In Exodus 31:13, Father God reveals Himself as Jehovah M'kaddesh, which means, "The Lord Who Sanctifies You." When I think of sanctification, I think of holiness, but God takes it even further than that. To be sanctified in and by Jesus Christ is to be set apart for a holy purpose. Not only am I made holy by simple faith in Jesus Christ, but I am called into a higher kingdom purpose. This gave my life a never-before-seen vision and purpose—a destiny—that transcended my humanity. When I was in bondage to my particular sin—way of thinking—I could see no further than the sin could take me. In my sin, there was no procreation. In my sin, there was no hope for true love as God had ordained it. In my sin, there was only hope for deeper depths of condemnation and fear of disease and ridicule of men. In my sin, there was no hope or future. To have Father God tell me He had made me holy and that I should see myself as holy and pure was quite revolutionary, but that was only the beginning of my revelation! He had a definite purpose for my existence. This new focus took the wind out of the sails of temptation for me in a dramatic way. My very real needs were now being met in the way God had intended them to be met all along: in relationship with Him. I am holy and set apart because He says so!

> For in it the righteousness of God is revealed from faith to faith; as it is written, "BUT THE RIGHTEOUS man shall live by faith." (Romans 1:17)

In God's Word, we find the details of an episode in the life of the patriarch Abraham. Abraham had finally been given a son in his old age, and when the boy, Isaac, was still a young man, the Lord directed Abraham to sacrifice him on the altar! Abraham, being a man of faith, reluctantly obeyed the Lord and took his son to the place as directed by God. Just as Abraham lifted the knife to sacrifice his son, the Lord intervened:

> But the angel of the LORD called to him from heaven and said, "Abraham, Abraham!" And he said, "Here I am." He said, "Do not stretch out your hand against the lad, and do nothing to him; for now I know that you fear God, since you have not withheld your son, your only son, from Me." Then Abraham raised his eyes and looked, and behold, behind him a ram caught in the thicket by his horns; and Abraham went and took the ram and offered him up for a burnt offering in the place of his son. Abraham called the name of that place The LORD Will Provide, as it is said to this day, "In the mount of the LORD it will be provided." (Genesis 22:11-14)

But the Lord did not stop there. He went on:

> Then the angel of the LORD called to Abraham a second time from heaven, and said, "By Myself I have sworn, declares the LORD, because you have done this thing and have not withheld your son, your only son, indeed I will greatly bless you, and I will greatly multiply your seed as the stars of the heavens and as the sand which is on the

seashore; and your seed shall possess the gate of their enemies. "In your seed all the nations of the earth shall be blessed, because you have obeyed My voice." (Genesis 22:15-18)

When I was confronted with the choice of following Jesus, He asked me for everything. Had I held back from Him, He could not bless me in the area I withheld from Him. When we hold on to a lie, we hold God's blessing at bay, in a sense. How can He fill with Truth something we fill with a lie? When I got honest with God about my greatest failures and shameful acts and thoughts, I effectively emptied myself—and He was given the freedom to fill those empty places with right thinking. The more I practiced right thinking the more freedom came into my life. The more freedom I experienced, the more my feelings changed. Why would we ever want to hide from God when rich blessings are the reward for our honest confession? What I discovered in that moment of clear thinking was that the very things the world promised—momentary pleasure, selfish ambition leading nowhere concrete, material possessions that would one day crumble into nothingness—were pathetic counterfeits to the richness of knowing Christ! In His economy, we are granted the riches of heaven by giving Him everything we have and are. God is, indeed, the best Provider!

One of the greatest Truths about who God is revealed to be is found in Judges 6:24, where the Father reveals Himself as Jehovah-Shalom: "The Lord Is Peace." In that account of Israeli history, a man named Gideon had been called of the Lord to lead God's people against the marauding Midianites and Amalekites. Rather than believe God that he could stand against the intruders, Gideon chose to hide in the wine press, choosing to winnow grain in order to save at least the food rather than to fight for the people! He saw himself as something less than the Father saw him. This is evident in the following passage:

The angel of the LORD appeared to him and said to him, "The LORD is with you, O valiant warrior." Then Gideon said to him, "O my lord, if the LORD is with us, why then has all this happened to us? And where are all His miracles which our fathers told us about, saying, 'Did not the LORD bring us up from Egypt?' But now the LORD has abandoned us and given us into the hand of

Midian." The LORD *looked at him and said, "Go in this your strength and deliver Israel from the hand of Midian. Have I not sent you?" (Judges 6:12-14)*

Like Gideon, I once believed myself a coward, controlled by fear, frozen by the lies of the enemy into a state of constant panic. Like Gideon, I used to blame God for getting me into the mess I was in rather than to see it was by my own choosing. Like Gideon, everything changed the moment I chose to believe God's Word. Gideon went on to find peace even before going to battle with the enemy. He and a small number of men routed the formidable foe and sent them packing! Like Gideon, once I believed and received God's peace, I was able to confront the liar and rout Him—and send him packing—all by virtue of believing and thinking the Truth of God's Word! I am a mighty man of valor, in spite of the lies of the enemy and in spite of whatever the world and its wisdom may say or do. I am who the Father says I am.

Of course, these are merely a few of the names God gives Himself in His Word, but they are important beginning steps to understanding who He is. It is by understanding who our Maker is that we come to have a roadmap to understanding who we are created to be—in spite of the way we feel. Feelings can change as thoughts are renewed. The name *Jesus* literally means, "The Lord Saves." How cool is that? Every name of God can be summarized in that one name: Jesus. And we need to be saved from sin, no doubt, but we also need to be saved from wrong thinking; saved from our own self.

Here is how drastic I became in my assault of stinkin' thinkin' as it relates to who my Father says He is. If I have the DNA of my Father flowing through my spiritual veins, this Truth not only affects how I view myself, but it informs me as to the reason of my existence. I am here for His glory and pleasure, not my own! I am to lead others to Jesus. I am to *be there* for others. I am to be a champion for and fight for the victory over sin of others. I am to see myself as a shepherd of those I am in relationship with and seek to lead people to green pasture and fresh water in the Lord. I am a conduit of God's healing power and love. I am called to walk in righteousness and have been set apart for a holy purpose, and I am called to lead others to that same righteous and holy identity in Christ. I am to be an agent of provision, meeting the spiritual needs of those I am in relationship with. I am an agent of God's peace. I am an ambassador for Christ on this planet. That changes everything!

> *Finally, brethren, whatever things are true, whatever things are noble, whatever things are just, whatever things are pure, whatever things are lovely, whatever things are of good report, if there is any virtue and if there is anything praiseworthy—meditate on these things. (Philippians 4:8)*

8

WHO I AM

How does one put on the Truth when the reality of his life says one thing about his identity, yet God calls him something new? What does one do if his feelings never change? What is ultimate Truth? We can argue over these questions all day long, but until we come to a firm grasp of where our foundation truly lies, we will always lack peace. As long as the wisdom of man is the foundation from which you base reality, your foundation lasts until the first failure of that wisdom— and have no doubt, man's strength always fades. *Always.* If feelings are what you rely on to confirm your identity, you are still operating from a man-centered worldview. If I identified myself by the way I feel from time to time, I would be an angry, vengeful, wounded, greedy, over-indulgent man, to say the least! Thank God He gave me a brand new identity and reminds me I have no right to call myself something my Father does not call me!

And just what is ultimate Truth? From God's point of view, it is His written Word. The holy Scripture. The Bible. As new creations, we are no longer made righteous by the Law of the Old Testament (Covenant). That Law was fulfilled by the work of the cross and sacrifice of Jesus Christ. We operate out of a New Covenant. Jesus fulfilled the Law and we are free to approach God through our faith in Jesus Christ. In fact, we are granted all the benefits of that Covenant because we have been made joint heirs of the kingdom again through faith in Jesus Christ. Here's what the Word says in this regard:

> *The Spirit Himself testifies with our spirit that we are children of God, and if children, heirs also, heirs of God and fellow heirs with Christ, if indeed we suffer with Him so that we may also be glorified with Him. (Romans 8:16-17)*

If we are joint heirs of God with Jesus Christ, then all that is made available to Jesus Christ is available to us, as well. Do you get that? All that Jesus has, *we* have! All the power He has been granted, *we* have been granted. All the blessings He has received, *we* are able to receive. All the power that raised Him from the dead is the same power God has given us. We have power over sin. We have power over temptation. We have power over our past failures. We have power over our present circumstances. We have power over our own thoughts. We have power over death. We have power over every choice we are faced with. We have the power to love to the degree that we believe we are loved. That is what ultimate Truth grants us. That is utter reality through faith in Jesus Christ. This is who you are, believer!

Just because we choose to disregard the Truth has no effect on its validity or staying power. My lack of understanding or ability to see what God sees never negates the Truth. That brings me great joy and peace as I pursue Him. If I believed everything that was said about me that is contrary to His Word, I would be relegated to deep, dark depression and stagnation. I simply respond to the Truth in faith, regardless of whether I feel like a new creation or not. That is what faith does. That is how a man or woman of faith responds. We respond out of the Truth in spite of how we feel. And speaking from my own experience, feelings always follow suit when I walk in the Truth of God's Word. *Always*. They may not unfold in my being instantaneously, but as I change my thoughts, I give way to new emotions. My attitudes change in the process, and these changes affect the way I behave. When I have success in my behavior, this produces even more healthy emotions and induces further righteous thinking. This whole new upward spiral floods in to replace the formerly downward cycle of my thoughts.

The Truth has the awesome ability to transcend any feeling or circumstance I face. The Truth sets me free from the snares of fleshly feelings and actually taps me into the emotions of my Creator. The Truth sets me free from the snares of hopelessness by taking my eyes off of me and my circumstances and placing my gaze upon the goal of my calling, Jesus Christ.

As a new creation learning to see myself as God sees me, I must also learn to see others the way he sees them. I can no longer judge people according to all I see, but I choose to judge them according to their destiny and true calling. In other words, when we see someone who is acting in a certain way we deem selfish or sinful, we need to see what Father God sees: He sees a lost sheep in need of guidance and love; he sees a fallen child in need of rescue. We need to view others the same way and as we do, we will come to appreciate all the more who the Father says we are. Remember, if it wasn't for the grace of God, I could just as easily be in their predicament.

> For the love of Christ controls us, having concluded this, that one died for all, therefore all died; and He died for all, so that they who live might no longer live for themselves, but for Him who died and rose again on their behalf. Therefore from now on we recognize no one according to the flesh; even though we have known Christ according to the flesh, yet now we know Him in this way no longer. (2 Corinthians 5:14-16)

With other believers I can make appeals for them to put an end to sinful behavior based upon their identity in Christ. When my own children were still at home, if I saw them sin—caught lying, for instance—I would say, "Son or daughter, you lied to me, but that is not who you are. You are not a liar. A new creation's true desire is to tell the truth. You are a truthful person; a portrait of God's grace to the world, like a trophy that declares the power of God to all who see you!" Just as I did with my children, I now do the same thing for those I am in relationship with, regardless of whether they are my children—or grandchildren—or not. That is what Truth and love born out of my identity demand.

In the last chapter, we focused on who Father God says He is (and what He calls Himself), revealing His character and nature. Let us go to the foundation of His Word once again and discover some specific things He calls us.

Who does the Father say you are? **He calls me a trophy grace.** This is my personal interpretation of what my life is to demonstrate about me. While this is not a scriptural term, it does express scriptural Truth. What is a trophy? A trophy is a tangible reminder of some great accomplishment or achievement. The redeemed life is a trophy or reminder to all who see of one of God's greatest achievements—you! Paul the apostle suffered much, yet he believed his sufferings and the display of God's grace to carry him through them had a profound purpose.

> ...*That the grace which is spreading to more and more people may cause the giving of thanks to abound to the glory of God.* (2 Corinthians 4:15)

We must learn to put off the old and put on the new of who we really are. In that way, we confront and deal with sin, yet we tear down only the sin and not the person. This is how we build one another up. This is how God builds us up. In this way, we each become testimonies of grace. **He calls me a letter, written to all mankind.**

> *You are our letter, written in our hearts, known and read by all men; being manifested that you are a letter of Christ, cared for by us, written not with ink but with the Spirit of the living God, not on tablets of stone but on tablets of human hearts.* (2 Corinthians 3:2-3)

As others see the changes God brings about in our lives, it is as if He has written a love letter for everyone who comes in contact with us to read. My life without Jesus spoke volumes. My redeemed life reads like a letter that was written with the greatest of care. My desire is that God be glorified for all He has done for me—so I open up that letter (my heart) for others to see and read. My desire is that, as they read, their lives are brought to a saving faith in Jesus Christ as well.

What do others see when they read our lives? Will we allow others to see and read, or will we hide what we have experienced of God? We have nothing to be ashamed of by being honest. Honesty is a byproduct of truth. Truth sets us—and others—free! Let us see beyond our own perceptions and see what we cannot always see. Let us see ourselves as the Father sees us. Let us see others as the Father does.

Who does the Father say I am? **He says I am a winner!** He gives me the strength to fight the good fight of faith and to run the race toward the goal for the prize of my highest calling. Though I fall, I get up and keep running. To win a race, I must run that race.

> *Do you not know that those who run in a race all run, but only one receives the prize? Run in such a way that you win. (1 Corinthians 9:24)*

The Word also says,

> *Let us lay aside every encumbrance, and the sin which so easily entangles us, and let us run with endurance the race that is set before us, fixing our eyes on Jesus, the author and perfecter of faith, who for the joy set before Him, endured the cross, despising the shame, and has sat down at the right hand of the throne of God. For consider Him who has endured such hostility by sinners against Himself, so that you may not grow weary and lose heart. (Hebrews 12:1-3)*

What is a failure? A failure is the one who falls and does not get back up. Either freedom is worth fighting for, or it's not! Falling does not determine one's identity. The Creator does that. I am not defined by past failure, present temptations, circumstances, or other people. I am who my Father says I am!

Who does the Father say I am? **He calls me a fighter!** I do not give up—I am tenacious concerning my desire to conquer sin and to glorify my Redeemer. I fight the good fight of faith by taking hold of the eternal life to which I am called, declaring the Truth to all who would see or hear—I am redeemed!

> *Fight the good fight of faith; take hold of the eternal life to which you were called, and you made the good confession in the presence of many witnesses. (1 Timothy 6:12)*

Father delights in me more than I in Him. His thoughts toward me outnumber the sands of the sea. Mine towards Him come nowhere near that!

How precious also are Your thoughts to me, O God!
How vast is the sum of them!
If I should count them, they would outnumber the sand.
When I awake, I am still with You. (Psalm 139:17-18)

I do not have to earn His acceptance or approval. I already have it by virtue of the redeeming work of Christ upon the cross. God's Word says that He has made us accepted in the Beloved—accepted in Christ!

In Him we have redemption through His blood, the forgiveness of our trespasses, according to the riches of His grace which He lavished on us. In all wisdom and insight. (Ephesians 1:7-8)

He calls me His bride and calls Jesus my bridegroom. One day, my truest identity will be fulfilled in the consummation of true oneness with Christ in the eternal glory of heaven. What joy and pleasure to know I do not have to wait until heaven to experience that joy. I am known by my God in a deeply personal and intimate way, and He allows me to know Him! This is my destiny: "that I may know Him and the power of His resurrection" (Philippians 3:10).

My ultimate destiny? To be all God has called me to be. The overcoming testimony of my life? A fragrant aroma.

But thanks be to God, who always leads us in His triumph in Christ, and manifests through us the sweet aroma of the knowledge of Him in every place. (2 Corinthians 2:14)

I am a treasure born of God's spirit to be given back to Him as a sacrifice of praise.

But we have this treasure in earthen vessels, so that the surpassing greatness of the power may be of God and not ourselves. (2 Corinthians 4:7)

We will be afflicted in this life—but we will not be crushed. We may be perplexed by the twists and turns of our life, but we will not despair because we have hope. We will be persecuted for the sake of righteousness, but we will never be forsaken. We may even be struck down because of our faith, but we cannot be destroyed! Why? Because this is part of our identity and destiny in Christ. This is who we are!

Therefore we do not lose heart, but though our outer man is decaying, yet our inner man is being renewed day by day. For momentary, light affliction is producing for us an eternal weight of glory far beyond all comparison, while we look not at the things which are seen, but at the things which are not seen; for the things which are seen are temporal, but the things which are not seen are eternal. (2 Corinthians 4:16-18)

Believer. This is your destiny. This is who you are called to be. I am so proud of you! Keep your eyes fixed upon Jesus. Enjoy the journey. Enjoy getting to know your God. I cannot wait until we have the time of eternity to share one another's stories of God's redemption. Remember this: Our God wastes nothing! He will not waste one moment of sorrow or suffering or pain or even one moment of personal failure. He is able to take what we give Him, regardless of what it is, and make something beautiful of it.

As for you, you meant evil against me, but God meant it for good in order to bring about this present result, to preserve many people alive. (Genesis 50:20)

And we know that God causes all things to work together for good to those who love God, to those who are called according to His purpose. (Romans 8:28)

Let us be constantly on the quest of renewing our mind in Christ. Let us remember the enemy wants our destruction, and that destruction begins in the thoughts he is able to plant in our minds. Let us not allow them to take root any longer. Let us make our mind good soil and be good receivers of God's Word. Let us be transformed!

Therefore I urge you, brethren, by the mercies of God, to present your bodies a living and holy sacrifice, acceptable to God, which is your spiritual service of worship. And do not be conformed to this world, but be transformed by the renewing of your mind, so that you may prove what the will of God is, that which is good and acceptable and perfect. (Romans 12:1-2)

9

DECLARATIONS

I f God's Word is foundational to our reality, we need to take it to heart. Did you know that we have the power of life on our very tongues? In the words we speak over our own lives?

> *Death and life are in the power of the tongue,*
> *And those who love it will eat its fruit. (Proverb 18:21)*

There is much to be said about the words we speak to ourselves. It is perfectly normal to realize that we talk to ourselves—even when we do not think we do. What do you think dreams are? We are talking to ourselves and we are conversing with God if we are people of faith—at all times! We are called to encourage ourselves in the Lord, just as King David did.

There was an episode in the life of King David in which he led his army into battle. While they were away, the wives and children of David and his men were taken captive by the enemy. When David's men realized what had happened, they blamed David and talked of stoning him. Here is how David responded:

> *Moreover David was greatly distressed because the people spoke of stoning him, for all the people were embittered, each one because of his sons and his daughters. But David strengthened himself in the LORD his God. (1 Samuel 30:6)*

King David encouraged *himself* in the Lord. He spoke the Truth to his own soul. In his own words,

Why are you in despair, O my soul?
And why have you become disturbed within me?
Hope in God, for I shall again praise Him
For the help of His presence. (Psalm 42:5)

Even when circumstances are beyond our control, we have the choice as to how we will respond. We always have a choice as to whether or not we will speak Truth to our own minds. In my own life, I have had several surgeries. After surgery, the pain meds wreak havoc upon my mind, leading me to hallucinate. In those moments, I would call out to Melinda and ask her to speak Truth to me—to give me something tangible to hold on to with my thoughts. She would begin speaking God's Truth to me out loud. As my mind took stock of what she was declaring, my mind suddenly came to peace, having a solid Truth to hold on to! This became our practice until the day I was able to be rid of the need for pain medication.

On the advent of the next surgery I faced, we were pre-emptive. My family made me a Truth Jar—a simple mason jar full of small bits of God's Truth written on card stock and folded. Whenever I found my mind wandering to despair after surgery, I was to reach into that jar and read those nits of Truth as needed. Without fail, all it took was reading one of those Truths and my mind was brought back to reality, reality being what God calls Truth.

We must learn to use the power of our own words just as King David did. We have the choice in how we talk to ourselves. We can speak either death or life; which sounds like the wiser choice to you? Here are some simple Truths to declare to your own soul in moments of metal anguish and self-doubt. Speak these Truths to your own soul as needed. This is who you are!

- I am dead to sin.

  Even so consider yourselves to be dead to sin, but alive to God in
  Christ Jesus. (Romans 6:11)

- I am born again.

   Since you have in obedience to the Truth purified your souls for a sincere love of the brethren, fervently love one another from the heart, for you have been born again not of seed which is perishable but imperishable, that is, through the living and enduring word of God. (1 Peter 1:22-23)

- I am cleansed by the blood.

   …let us draw near with a sincere heart in full assurance of faith, having our hearts sprinkled clean from an evil conscience and our bodies washed with pure water. (Hebrews 10:22)

- I am alive to God.

   Even so consider yourselves to be dead to sin, but alive to God in Christ Jesus. (Romans 6:11)

- I am a victor, destined to win.

   Do you not know that those who run in a race all run, but only one receives the prize? Run in such a way that you may win. Everyone who competes in the games exercises self-control in all things. They then do it to receive a perishable wreath, but we an imperishable. Therefore I run in such a way, as not without aim; I box in such a way, as not beating the air; but I discipline my body and make it my slave, so that, after I have preached to others, I myself will not be disqualified. (1 Corinthians 9:24-27)

- I am a child of destiny and purpose.

   "For I know the plans that I have for you," declares the LORD, "plans for welfare and not for calamity to give you a future and a hope." (Jeremiah 29:11)

- I am eternally His.

   For you have been bought with a price: therefore glorify God in your body. (1 Corinthians 6:20)

- I am found.

"He who has found his life will lose it, and he who has lost his life for My sake will find it." —Jesus (Matthew 10:39)

- I am free.

"So if the Son makes you free, you will be free indeed." —Jesus (John 8:36)

- I am holy and righteous.

*But by His doing you are in Christ Jesus, who became to us wisdom from God, and righteousness and sanctification, and redemption, so that, just as it is written, "*LET HIM WHO BOASTS, BOAST IN THE LORD.*" (1 Corinthians 1:30-31)*

- I am an overcomer.

You are from God, little children, and have overcome them; because greater is He who is in you than he who is in the world. (1 John 4:4)

- I am redeemed.

Christ redeemed us from the curse of the Law, having become a curse for us... (Galatians 3:13)

- I am crowned with victory.

Blessed is a man who perseveres under trial; for once he has been approved, he will receive the crown of life which the Lord has promised to those who love Him. (James 1:12)

- I am restored.

The law of the LORD *is perfect, restoring the soul;*
The testimony of the LORD *is sure, making wise the simple.*
(Psalm 19:7)

...if indeed you have heard Him and have been taught in Him, just as truth is in Jesus, that, in reference to your former manner of life, you lay aside the old self, which is being corrupted in accordance with the lusts of deceit, and that you be renewed in the spirit of your mind, (Ephesians 4:21-23)

- I am resurrected to new life.

Therefore we have been buried with Him through baptism into death, so that as Christ was raised from the dead through the glory of the Father, so we too might walk in newness of life. For if we have become united with Him in the likeness of His death, certainly we shall also be in the likeness of His resurrection, knowing this, that our old self was crucified with Him, in order that our body of sin might be done away with, so that we would no longer be slaves to sin. (Romans 6:4-6)

- I am a new creation.

Therefore if anyone is in Christ, he is a new creature; the old things passed away; behold, new things have come. (2 Corinthians 5:17)

- I am a servant of the Most High God.

"But the greatest among you shall be your servant." —Jesus (Matthew 23:11)

"If anyone serves Me, he must follow Me; and where I am, there My servant will be also; if anyone serves Me, the Father will honor him." —Jesus (John 12:26)

- I am a mighty warrior.

But thanks be to God, who always leads us in triumph in Christ, and manifests through us the sweet aroma of the knowledge of Him in every place. (2 Corinthians 2:14)

For though we walk in the flesh, we do not war according to the flesh, for the weapons of our warfare are not of the flesh, but

*divinely powerful for the destruction of fortresses. We are destroying
speculations and every lofty thing raised up against the knowledge
of God, and we are taking every thought captive to the obedience
of Christ, and we are ready to punish all disobedience, whenever
your obedience is complete. (2 Corinthians 10:3-6)*

I am an ambassador for Christ.

*Therefore, we are ambassadors for Christ, as though God were
making an appeal through us; we beg you on behalf of Christ, be
reconciled to God. (2 Corinthians 5:20)*

I am chosen by God. I am a priest. I am royalty. I belong to God!

*But you are A CHOSEN RACE, A ROYAL PRIESTHOOD, A HOLY
NATION, A PEOPLE FOR GOD'S OWN POSSESSION, so that you
may proclaim the excellencies of Him who has called you out of
darkness into His marvelous light. (1 Peter 2:9)*

I am a receiver of visions and dreams.

*"AND IT SHALL BE IN THE LAST DAYS," God says,
"THAT I WILL POUR FORTH OF MY SPIRIT ON ALL MANKIND;
AND YOUR SONS AND YOUR DAUGHTERS SHALL PROPHESY,
AND YOUR YOUNG MEN SHALL SEE VISIONS,
AND YOUR OLD MEN SHALL DREAM DREAMS." (Acts 2:17)*

I am a letter of grace.

*You are our letter, written in our hearts, known and read by all men;
being manifested that you are a letter of Christ, cared for by us, written
not with ink but with the Spirit of the living God, not on tablets of
stone but on tablets of human hearts. (2 Corinthians 3:2-3)*

I am a minister of reconciliation, leading others to be reconciled
with God!

*Now all these things are from God, who reconciled us to Himself
through Christ and gave us the ministry of reconciliation, namely,*

that God was in Christ reconciling the world to Himself, not counting their trespasses against them, and He has committed to us the word of reconciliation. (2 Corinthians 5:18-19)

- I am a delight to my God.

For whom the LORD loves He reproves,
Even as a father corrects the son in whom he delights. (Proverbs 3:12)
The LORD your God in your midst,
The Mighty One, will save;
He will rejoice over you with gladness,
He will quiet you with His love,
He will rejoice over you with singing. (Zephaniah 3:17 NKJV)

- I am accepted.

…to the praise of the glory of His grace, by which He made us accepted in the Beloved. (Ephesians 1:6)

- I am a kingdom seeker!

"But seek first His kingdom and His righteousness, and all these things will be added to you." —Jesus (Matthew 6:33)

But from there you will seek the LORD your God, and you will find Him if you search for Him with all your heart and all your soul. (Deuteronomy 4:29)

10

DO NOT WALK ALONE

One of the most devious lies the enemy uses to defeat us is the lie that we are alone. He wants us to believe we are alone in the battle; that we are alone against the temptations; that we are alone in our pain; that we are alone in our shame; that we are alone in life—utterly alone. He knows that if we believe we are alone, then we will feel alone—and if we feel alone, then we will act as if we believe we are alone, often isolating ourselves away from the very ones God has brought to help us! Who does the wolf go after? The weak. The straggler. The lone sheep, separated from the protection of the flock.

The guilt and shame sin produces causes us to walk in pride more often than not. What else could you call it when you fear what others might think of you for confessing your sin? Only pride would keep you isolated. It would be like suffering a major health issue and going to the doctor. The first thing the doctor would ask would be, "Can you show me where it hurts?" If we responded with, "I can't allow someone else to see that. What would people think?" Such a response does not lead to healing. It leads to death. Do not confuse shame and guilt with pride. Pride keeps you from honest confession. Honest confession leads to Truth—and Truth sets you free!

How do I know these things? I speak from personal experience. When I was a younger man, fear of what others thought—pride—kept me from being honest. The living of lies and performance to keep others from asking questions became layer upon layer of what I thought was self-preservation. In actuality, these were layers of death! It took one moment of honesty to free me from that fear. Until that moment, I was wrapped up in self-pity brought on by loneliness. Out of the mentality that I must protect myself from others, I chose to separate myself from relationships. We were not created to walk alone. We were created—wired for—relationships. Without relationships, there is no life.

The Sea of Galilee in Israel is full of life. It receives rain and runoff from the surrounding hills. That same water, full of life, flows all the way to the Dead Sea. The Dead Sea receives the same water, yet it's *dead*! How can that be? Even though it receives water from the Sea of Galilee, it has no outflow. There is no give and take. There is no life because it only takes in and gives nothing back. As new creations in Christ, we are intended to thrive and flourish as we walk relationally with God and with others.

When I was caught within those layers of hiding and aloneness, I was right where the enemy wanted me. I let very little of myself out to others, disclosing nothing but surface details about my life. Safe. I let no one in for fear of being found out, exposed to the light of day. Although I felt I was protecting myself, I was actually feeding the flames of death and destruction in my own life. Let me tell you about the night that all began to change.

When I was fresh out of college, my plan was to go on to seminary, but the Lord had another plan for me. Through a series of events, I found myself living in Oklahoma City with my friend Chuck, and his mother, Beverly. Chuck had befriended me in college and had encouraged me to seek Jesus and to seek to pursue my dream of writing music. Because of my wretched state of self-loathing, Chuck was constantly talking me off of the emotional ledge I often found myself on. He was speaking life to me and I was receiving it—but I was giving nothing back. To do so leads to stagnation—and that would be a great way to describe my state of mind at the time.

One night during such a time of me expressing depression and stinkin' thinkin' due to my circumstances, Chuck very calmly said, "Dennis, I need to talk with you." I had not expected to hear such gravity in a tone that had given, up until that moment, any reason for alarm or fear. [The following portion is excerpted from my book, *Sing Over Me:*]

That night I could tell he had something on his mind...just by the way he was extra kind to me...extra attentive to my feelings about everything...extra encouraging. After dinner, we settled in the living room and, as was typical for our evenings, went to the piano to sing some of the songs I was writing in those days. All was well in my mind. The music flowed easily. The very atmosphere was peaceful and serene...like I didn't have a care in the world. And my friend was so gracious to me. Chuck was always kind in all his ways—but for some reason, he was extra sensitive to my mood that night.

After singing a few songs, we began to talk. Talking with Chuck was always so freeing and refreshing to me, full of encouraging words as well as words of challenge. He was always challenging me to go deeper in the things of God, and he was very sensitive when it came to sharing things God had impressed upon his heart for me. I could not help but think of the dream he had that set me on my current journey—that sent me to live with him. So whenever Chuck said he felt God had something for him to share with me, I was all ears. And tonight was no different.

"I have something I need to share with you, Dennis," he began.

"Sure," I said. "Go ahead."

Hesitating for a few seconds, like a wise man does, weighing his thoughts with discernment as how best to express them, I could tell that whatever Chuck had to say to me was pressing down heavily upon his heart.

"I've heard some things about you."

I froze. "What have you heard?" I asked.

I could now see anguish on Chuck's face but felt a deep compassion emanating from him as well. Looking me eye to eye, he said, "I know you're struggling with homosexuality."

In utter shock and disbelief that my secret had been spilled—and then filled with simultaneous rage and humiliation to know that my friend had heard the news from someone else—I burst from the room and out the front door, running as fast as I possibly could into the night. I ran and I ran and I ran, thinking all the while my *life is over!' I ran in desperation, ran on the adrenaline the shame of being found out and being confronted by one of my best friends had sent coursing through my body. Crying and shaking and feeling completely humiliated, I continued to run for several minutes. And then I stopped.*

As if a glass of cold, icy water had been suddenly thrown into my face, I was brought back to reality with this thought: where am I going? Where am I running to? What do I do now? I have no place left to turn. My best friend, whose home and presence had been a refuge for me, were suddenly gone. Assuming Chuck would have nothing to do with me...that his reason for telling me he knew about my secret was because he would need me to leave his home...I decided to just not go back. But still the question, where do I go now? kept playing over and over in my mind.

Sobbing uncontrollably now, I felt so helpless and alone. In the middle of a dark street in the middle of the night somehow seemed very appropriate to my life. Like the epitome of irony, the very thing I longed for—to be known completely—was the very thing that had now ushered me into what I, that moment, considered the deepest abyss my soul had ever gotten to...and I thought I had felt hopeless so many times before...but now *somehow felt like the end of the road—the real deal. Alone. Abandoned. Helpless. Without hope. And I stood there frozen at the edge of a cliff.*

I didn't know I could cry so deeply. I didn't know I could still feel so deeply. I had not expected this tonight. The night had been going so well. Why did it have to end this way? Wailing now, I began to cry out, "Why, Lord? Why?" and then the moaning grew deeper as the cry changed to, "Father, if you are real...if You are even there...I need You to speak to me! If ever I've needed you, it is now! Please speak to me!"

Somehow, simply uttering those words calmed my soul. Somehow, admitting I was helpless brought me to the place of complete brokenness and humility. Somehow, I knew I had no other hope if He did not speak. And it didn't take long...

The night was dark yet the sky was bright, illuminated by a full moon. I had not noticed the moon until that moment, so consumed with my pain I had been. So self-focused that I had not noticed the two clouds in the sky that now drew my attention. Without realizing what I was doing, I began to think about the days as a child out on the farm when I would just lie down in the grass and watch the clouds go by. Many hours were spent in those days looking to the clouds for images and shapes of creatures and people. I recalled dinosaurs and horses, sailing ships and serpents. For a few brief seconds I was somehow taken back to those days. To feel the innocence and wonder of a child was at once soothing to my grieving soul. And then I was shaken back to the present reality. To the two clouds, their shapes very evident in the moonlit sky.

At first I could not believe what I was seeing. Didn't want to put my hope in something not real. But the clouds were real and had very definite shapes. Recognizable shapes. Life-shaking shapes. And as if taken by unseen hands, my face was directed to look fully at what was transpiring in the heavens above me.

I was first drawn to the larger of the two clouds. There was no mistaking the image of an old man with a beard. With definition of features, the face was loving and welcoming—and inviting. I could not release my gaze on the figure, so full of love and acceptance it was. And then my face was directed to the smaller cloud. Amazed at what I was seeing, this cloud looked like a small lamb. A sheep. A wounded sheep in need of love and care. And as if on some cosmic cue, the old man cloud began to catch up to the little lamb cloud, as if it were pursing the broken little sheep. And then?

The old man cloud began to consume the little lamb cloud within itself! They became one! I could not believe what I was seeing...but hadn't I just asked the Lord to speak to me? And now this?!

Flooding with all manner of good thoughts, my mind began to calm down and peace began to flood my mind. Suddenly I knew what Father was saying. "This is what I want to do with and for you, son. I want to consume you. Consume your brokenness. Love you. Bind up your wounds. Heal your broken heart."

It was in that moment that I "heard," not in an audible voice, but rather in an impression on my mind, "Go back and face your friend. He is waiting for you. You can trust Me." So I went back home. It was a long walk...not because of the distance, just because I was so afraid of what my friend may say and do. Even though I had felt I had just heard the Lord speak to me, I was still so full of fear I could hardly function. All I know is that somehow the Lord gave me the strength to head home.

Approaching the door, I thought I would be able to sneak in without Chuck noticing. But he hadn't moved from where I had last seen him! He had been waiting all that time! Just that realization—that he had waited—sent chills of peace through my veins. It is one thing for people to tell you they love you—and quite another for them to prove their love. In that moment I gained a deeper understanding of what real love was supposed to look like. Real loves requires the laying down of life. Sacrifice. And Chuck was about to lay down his life for me in a deeply profound way.

Slinking into the room, head bowed dejectedly, I could not bring myself to even look at him, so wracked with shame I was. In his wisdom, my friend did not try to get me to look him right in the eye, but wisely waited to allow the honesty of the moment and the depth of his love and commitment to me restore me to a feeling of pure acceptance—void of shame.

He simply asked me to sit down...because he had something he wanted to share with me. Expecting complete rejection, I girded myself for the worst. But with the very tone of his voice and the compassion with which he spoke, I was set immediately at ease as I took my seat near him.

"Dennis," he began. "I'll be honest with you. I do not know how to help you. All I know is I know the answer."

At once I was flooded with feelings of hope...and I began to let my guard down. All I said was, "You know the answer? What's the answer?"

His answer was short and unexpectedly to the point. "Jesus is the Answer."

As I sat there stunned and actually a bit incredulous in attitude, I said, "Jesus is the answer? I've heard that my whole life! I've asked Him to change me time and time again...and nothing's ever happened! How is Jesus the Answer? I've heard it all before."

"Not like this, you haven't," he declared confidently.

"What do you mean?" I asked.

What he said next took my breath away...and still does to this day whenever I remember that moment. "Though I do not know any magic formula or know what steps might be required for your freedom from this, I do believe Jesus is the Answer. And here's what I mean by that. I believe so much that He is what you need to be free that I am willing to walk toward Jesus with you...as long as it takes...whatever it takes. When you fall down, I will not kick you. I will not say, 'I told you so.' You know what I'll do? I'll help you up every time."

By now, my tears had again begun to flow. As if being bathed in pure love and acceptance, though I did not know it at the time, I was having a real-life personal demonstration of the act of love...the laying down of life. But he wasn't quite through.

"Dennis, not only will I walk with you as long as it takes. If you need a shoulder to cry on, use mine. If you need someone to yell at when the frustration grows too burdensome, yell at me. I can handle it. Let's just walk toward Jesus together."

It was in that moment that God restored hope in my soul...and it began to burn like a fire within me. As never before, I began to seek Jesus, still focused on my performance, not quite understanding yet that God's love for me was in no way connected to my performance. But at least now I didn't feel so alone. Finally I had someone who, though they might not have gone through exactly what I'd gone through in my life, they were sensitive enough to walk through the recovery of a broken heart with me.

By the way, Chuck kept his word. He has walked through the past thirty-two years with me...toward Jesus. Love looks like my friend, Chuck.

My point? God wired us for relationship with Himself and with one another. We need one another. Life is lived when life is exchanged. True intimacy is when we understand that God is waiting for us to say to Him, "Father, here is my heart. Into me, see." True relationship happens when we understand that in that same moment, He is saying to us, "Son or daughter, here is My heart. Into me, see." Without relationship, we are like ships floundering about on the ocean of life with no anchor and no sail and no rudder and...you get the idea. We are left stranded, exposed to the elements (lies of the enemy), and trying to make our way with nothing but futility being the result.

Without people to help us walk through and navigate life, the enemy has us right where he wants us. Alone and floundering, like a wounded sheep separated from the safety of the flock, he is able to sweep in like a ravenous wolf and devour our mind with negative thoughts. Without someone else to speak into our lives, we have a very limited perspective—especially as it pertains to our own lives.

There is a reason God's Word speaks so much about the need to surround ourselves with the body...because life flows from cell to cell. Nutrients flow from cell to cell. Healing flows from cell to cell. Life-giving oxygen flows from cell to cell. Every part of the body of Christ needs the other parts of the body.

...so that there may be no division in the body, but that the members may have the same care for one another. And if one member suffers,

all the members suffer with it; if one member is honored, a. members rejoice with it. Now you are Christ's body, and individua. members of it. (1 Corinthians 12:25-27)

Take a few minutes to read the following passages of God's W _d that communicate the wisdom of the Truth that we need one another relationally. I would strongly suggest you begin asking the Lord to bring godly men and women into your life who you can share life with because you need people...but remember this: people need who you are and need what you have as well! Humble yourself and seek out relationship with other believers.

But He gives a greater grace. Therefore it says, "GOD IS OPPOSED TO THE PROUD, BUT GIVES GRACE TO THE HUMBLE." Submit therefore to God. Resist the devil and he will flee from you. Draw near to God and He will draw near to you. Cleanse your hands, you sinners; and purify your hearts, you double-minded. (James 4:6-8)

And if one can overpower him who is alone, two can resist him. A cord of three strands is not quickly torn apart. (Ecclesiastes 4:12)

Where there is no guidance the people fall, But in abundance of counselors there is victory. (Proverbs 11:14)

For by wise guidance you will wage war, And in abundance of counselors there is victory. (Proverbs 24:6)

But encourage one another day after day, as long as it is still called "Today," so that none of you will be hardened by the deceitfulness of sin. (Hebrews 3:13)

Therefore encourage one another and build up one another, just as you also are doing. (1 Thessalonians 5:11)

The things which you have heard from me in the presence of many witnesses, entrust these to faithful men who will be able to teach others also. (2 Timothy 2:2)

11

AUTHORITY OF THE BELIEVER

M ake no mistake, we are at war. We are in the spiritual battle of and for our lives.

Be of sober spirit, be on the alert. Your adversary, the devil, prowls around like a roaring lion, seeking someone to devour. (1 Peter 5:8)

The mistake far too many new creations make is feeling they are helpless to do anything about the culture in which they live. The big mistake is believing their citizenship is of this world. We are aliens in a strange land simply by virtue of our new nature. When we were born again we became exiles—but that is a good and grand thing because that means we are citizens of the kingdom of God!

"If you were of the world, the world would love its own; but because you are not of the world, but I chose you out of the world, because of this the world hates you." —Jesus (John 15:19)

So then you are no longer strangers and aliens, but you are fellow citizens with the saints, and are of God's household, having been built on the foundation of the apostles and prophets, Christ Jesus Himself being the corner stone, in whom the whole building, being fitted together, is growing into a holy temple in the Lord, in whom you also are being built together into a dwelling of God in the Spirit. (Ephesians 2:19-22)

Even though we are not citizens of this world, we need to remember that people who do not know Jesus are not the enemy. People are not our enemy! The *enemy*—the liar—is the enemy! We are at war with the spirit of darkness no matter how much the world mocks us. We must recognize and realize that we must fight that battle. And even though we must fight, and fighting involves strategy and stamina, we have been wired—as new creations—for both. Not only that, but we have been given the necessary weapons with which to wage this war. And not only that, but we have been given the authority to do so. We have been given authority *over* the enemy.

STRATEGY: WE WIN!

The good news about the war we are in is that we win! No matter what, we win! So replace the lie that condemns you as a loser and put on the Truth of God's Word. You are destined to win! We may have losses and fail from time to time in our thought life, but we must have this attitude: one lost battle does not equal the loss of the entire war. The only failure is the man or woman who falls and simply decides to not get back up. A victor just keeps getting back up and heading for the finish line: toward Jesus!

And they overcame him because of the blood of the Lamb and because of the word of their testimony, and they did not love their life even when faced with death. (Revelations 12:11)

In faith, I have overcome even my past and even my old ways of thinking by appropriating the blood of Jesus Christ as having paid my debt in full. As I speak of what God has done for me—as I testify to His power and love in my life—that very appropriation of faith brings me even more renewal of thought and more and more victory. Because I have no doubt about His love for me, fear has been taken out of the equation as well.

But thanks be to God, who always leads us in triumph in Christ, and manifests through us the sweet aroma of the knowledge of Him in every place. (2 Corinthians 2:14)

For we do not have a high priest who cannot sympathize with our weaknesses, but One who has been tempted in all things as we are, yet without sin. (Hebrews 4:15)

Just in case you were wondering, Jesus was tempted in every manner, just as you and I are tempted. Temptation does not equal sin. Temptation becomes an opportunity to choose the way we think. We are never to be defined by the things that tempt us. We are meant to be defined by our Maker! Knowing Jesus understands what I have been faced with gives me hope and grace and faith—and a new way of thinking about the things that tempt me. With every temptation He makes a way of escape. That means I have yet another opportunity to seek the Lord for the way of escape. Suddenly, my thoughts are taken off of me and placed on hope. When Jesus was tempted, what did He do? He chose to put off the lie and put on the Truth of God's Word. We can do the same.

No temptation has overtaken you but such as is common to man; and God is faithful, who will not allow you to be tempted beyond what you are able, but with the temptation will provide the way of escape also, so that you will be able to endure it. (1 Corinthians 10:13)

But He answered and said, "It is written, 'MAN SHALL NOT LIVE ON BREAD ALONE, BUT ON EVERY WORD THAT PROCEEDS OUT OF THE MOUTH OF GOD.'" —Jesus (Matthew 4:4)

And he answered, "YOU SHALL LOVE THE LORD YOUR GOD WITH ALL YOUR HEART, AND WITH ALL YOUR SOUL, AND WITH ALL YOUR STRENGTH, AND WITH ALL YOUR MIND; AND YOUR NEIGHBOR AS YOURSELF." —Jesus (Luke 10:27)

Part of our strategy as new creations in the battles we face is knowing that regardless of what we are faced with, God has made a way. We are afflicted, but we are not crushed. The world around us walks in despair, but we have hope. We will be persecuted, but never forgotten.

Even if we are struck down, we can never be destroyed! What a great strategy our God has given us. Let us change the way we think and let victory be our way of thinking!

> *But we have this treasure in earthen vessels, so that the surpassing greatness of the power will be of God and not from ourselves; we are afflicted in every way, but not crushed; perplexed, but not despairing; persecuted, but not forsaken; struck down, but not destroyed; always carrying about in the body the dying of Jesus, so that the life of Jesus also may be manifested in our body. (2 Corinthians 4:7-10)*

STAMINA

> *Consider it all joy, my brethren, when you encounter various trials, knowing that the testing of your faith produces endurance. And let endurance have its perfect result, so that you may be perfect and complete, lacking in nothing. (James 1:2-4)*

I will be honest with you. From time to time, I grow tired of the battle. Not the battle for my own thoughts, that's a battle that I find joyful because it affords me constant companionship with Jesus. My weariness stems from the constant belittling from the world. How many times can one hear the words, "You're doing more damage than good by telling someone they can change"? How many times can one be called delusional or a hater or a bigot or worse before it begins to weigh on them? How many times can one be told by the Christian music business to stop sharing your story because we don't know how to market you? Personally, when I feel overwhelmed by such thoughts, I take steps to clear the clouds of thought by ceasing. I stop listening to the hateful voices. I stop watching the evening news. I stop allowing the culture to invade my thought life. I withdraw into seclusion and restore my soul.

My understanding is that my faith will be tested, by both the church and the world. But that very faith leads me to endurance—standing through thick or thin due to the grace afforded me by Christ. The result? My needs are met and I can go back and face the world for another season of battle. Remember, we are not in a sprint. We are running a marathon...and we have been equipped for the long haul.

WEAPONS

For though we walk in the flesh, we do not war according to the flesh, for the weapons of our warfare are not of the flesh, but divinely powerful for the destruction of fortresses. We are destroying speculations and every lofty thing raised up against the knowledge of God, and we are taking every thought captive to the obedience of Christ, and we are ready to punish all disobedience, whenever your obedience is complete. (2 Corinthians 10:3-6)

For the word of God is living and active and sharper than any two-edged sword, and piercing as far as the division of soul and spirit, of both joints and marrow, and able to judge the thoughts and intentions of the heart. (Hebrews 4:12)

My weaponry is simple. I have a sword. It is vital that every believer put on the Truth of God's Word. Not only does this accomplish the victory in our minds over our own thoughts, but it affords us victory over the enemy! Jesus used the Word when He was tempted. We can do no less! Memorize it. Put on its Truth in thought and concept. Wear it. Allow it to permeate your thoughts. Allow the Word to be the filter of your mind, and use it. Often. Loudly. Boldly. It is your sword, believer.

Submit yourselves therefore to God. Resist the devil, and he will flee from you. (James 4:7 NKJV)

ARMOR

Put on the full armor of God, so that you will be able to stand firm against the schemes of the devil. For our struggle is not against flesh and blood, but against the rulers, against the powers, against the world forces of this darkness, against the spiritual forces of wickedness in the heavenly places. Therefore, take up the full armor of god, so that you will be able to resist in the evil day, and having done everything, to stand firm. Stand firm therefore, HAVING GIRDED YOUR LOINS WITH TRUTH, and HAVING PUT ON THE BREASTPLATE OF RIGHTEOUSNESS, and having shod YOUR FEET WITH THE PREPARATION OF THE GOSPEL OF PEACE; in addition to all, taking up the shield of faith with which you will be able to extinguish all the flaming arrows of the evil one. and take THE HELMET OF SALVATION, and the sword of the Spirit, which is the word of God. (Ephesians 6:11-17)

When God calls us to be born again, He offers us the armor we will need for each and every battle we will ever face. We are granted this armor in the moment of salvation, but we must learn to appropriate it into our very thought-life, be aware that it is there—or we will never use it to its full purpose and power.

Gird your spiritual loins. Just as we take steps to protect the life-giving part of who we are as humans—protective athletic cups, armor, padding, etc.—we are to protect our thought-life. In human physiology, the loins are where the seeds of life emanate from. This is a picture of how we are to guard over our own life—the way we think—with Truth. Renew the mind and we guard over life.

Cover your heart with the breastplate of righteousness. This means we simply call ourselves what God calls us. Refer to the chapter on declarations. My personal rule is that I cannot call myself something my Father does not call me. This keeps my heart covered.

Shod your feet with the Gospel of Peace. In other words, we are not here for our own glory or pleasure, but for His. We are ministers of reconciliation. We are ambassadors for Christ. Every step we take is a part of this mission—to bring others the life and light of Jesus Christ!

Take up the shield of faith. This is simply walking in the Truth that God is in control, regardless.

Put on the helmet of salvation. This is simply covering one's mind with the Truth that they are born again. Saved from sin. Utterly, irrevocably purchased by and belonging to God. Again, the mind is covered and thoughts are renewed.

The sword of the Spirit. The Word of God. Need I say more?

AUTHORITY

Jesus summoned His twelve disciples and gave them authority over unclean spirits, to cast them out, and to heal every kind of disease and every kind of sickness. (Matthew 10:1)

And Jesus came up and spoke to them, saying, "All authority has been given to Me in heaven and on earth." (Matthew 28:18)

As disciples of Christ, we are commanded to go and make more disciples. Because we are disciples of Christ, He has given us authority—the right and power—to wield His Truth to and in the world around us. Our job is to believe it and receive it, and to walk in it. And how do we walk in it? We put off the thoughts of the enemy that would persuade us otherwise, and we put on the Truth that we *do* have the authority Jesus granted to us along with those first disciples.

"Behold, I have given you authority to tread on serpents and scorpions, and over all the power of the enemy, and nothing will injure you."
—Jesus (Luke 10:19)

Not only do we have authority over the enemy, we do not fight alone! We must remember this. We do not fight alone. It is a good thing to band with other believers in agreement as we face the lies of the enemy. When I am embattled with stinkin' thinkin', I always let others know. Always! This not only emboldens my own heart, but it puts the enemy on notice and in flight.

And if one can overpower him who is alone, two can resist him. A cord of three strands is not quickly torn apart. (Ecclesiastes 4:12)

We were never intended to be lone sheep. Wisdom calls for us to bind our hearts with others in the body of Christ. This ensures wisdom and victory—especially in our thought-life.

Where there is no guidance the people fall,
But in abundance of counselors there is victory. (Proverbs 11:14)
For by wise guidance you will wage war,
And in abundance of counselors there is victory. (Proverbs 24:6)

But encourage one another day after day, as long as it is still called "Today," so that none of you will be hardened by the deceitfulness of sin. (Hebrews 3:13)

Therefore encourage one another and build up one another, just as you also are doing. (1 Thessalonians 5:11)

Do you want victory over your thoughts? Do you want to win? Do you want to win the battle for your mind? Put on the Truth of God's Word!

Finally, brethren, whatever is true, whatever is honorable, whatever is right, whatever is pure, whatever is lovely, whatever is of good repute, if there is any excellence and if anything worthy of praise, dwell on these things. (Philippians 4: 8)

12

THE HEALING OF
MEMORIES

There really is always more. Since my initial healing, life has become less of a burden and more of an adventure. I have learned to stop seeing life through the lens of the world—or through the lens of the enemy of God—and learned to see each and every situation and circumstance through the lens of the kingdom of God. What does that mean? I want to see life from God's perspective rather than solely from my human perspective. From a human point of view, I see a lot of hurt and failure and death and destruction, but from God's point of view, I see a lot of healing and triumph and life and restoration! I can either see what God sees and respond with hope, or I can see what the enemy wants me to see and walk in despair.

How did I learn this? While still at the church in Oklahoma City, Pastor Jerry taught us to pray using the Lord's Prayer as a pattern.

> *Pray, then, in this way: "Our Father who is in heaven, Hallowed be Your name. Your kingdom come. Your will be done, On earth as it is in heaven. Give us this day our daily bread. And forgive us our debts, as we also have forgiven our debtors. And do not lead us into temptation, but deliver us from evil. For Yours is the kingdom and the power and the glory forever. Amen." —Jesus (Matthew 6:9-13)*

For eight years we gathered at 6 a.m. Monday through Friday to pray, and I helped lead that prayer time. As we asked the Lord to bring His kingdom into our lives in a tangible way, we began to experience freedom and insight to successful living that I had never experienced or seen before. During that time, it began to dawn on me the reality of the words of Jesus in Matthew 6:33 that says, "But seek first His kingdom and His righteousness, and all these things will be added to you." To seek to know the kingdom, I reasoned, I had better be seeking to know the King of that kingdom, Jesus Christ! So my journey became even more intimate and even more liberating in those days. Overcoming same sex attraction became such a small portion of my life because I began to discover that the true needs of my life were more basic than the sexual temptations I experienced that even those fleeting temptations would wane if I met my needs through Jesus.

As the years went on and I deepened my walk with God, the freedom I experienced went to places I had only dreamed of being possible. It was as if what I had experienced on the night of November 7, 1981, was merely the beginning of my liberation. That night the doors were blown off of my personal hell and prison. What transpired in the years to come has been nothing less than Father tearing down the prison walls in ways I did not even know I needed.

Even though I had been walking in freedom since 1981, the realization of the massive extent of that freedom was yet to dawn on me. During the years of 1989 and 1990, I was telling my story more and more in public forums. With each sharing of that story, I felt a bit freer than the previous time. It was amazing to experience...yet I still had moments of despair and depression and anxiety. This was somewhat bewildering to me because I considered myself free. If I was so free, why did I still battle such things? After all, I knew who I was in Christ, and I knew whose I was as His child!

By this time, I had become fully aware that my battleground was not my physical body, but rather my *mind*. For this reason, I had come to trust the Lord in faith even when my feelings did not match up to what I knew to be truth. As I sought the Lord about this one day, I heard Him say, "Son, what are you thinking about when despairing, depressing, anxious thoughts come?"

That was an easy one to answer. "Lord, why did you allow homosexuality in my life? Where were you when I was five years old and that man exposed himself to me? You say in your Word that you will never leave me and never forsake me...but it seems like you did. And how about when my grandmother died? You left me utterly alone. And why did my dad never tell me he loved me until after I was married? And that incident with my college mentor? Where were you in that?"

Every depressing and despairing anxious thought was attached to a memory of wounding in my past. "What do I do with those thoughts, Father?"

"You give them to Me, son. Make a list of all the times you feel I have forsaken or forgotten you and I will show you my point of view when the time is right. Just make your list...and trust Me."

So I did. That list became several pages long. Single line memories. Single moments of hurt. Moments of betrayal. Moments of humiliation. Moments of shame. Moments I had carried since childhood. After my list was complete, I felt exhausted yet one step closer to God in honest intimacy. Lighter. Freer. Yet still lost in a fog of wondering how and when God would reveal His Truth to me. After I made my list and felt I had gotten everything out in the open, I gave the list to Father and asked Him to show me His point of view whenever He would. I did not have to wait long.

Two weeks passed and I had honestly not thought much about the list. Just making it had taken away some of the feelings I had been dealing with. In addition, I had been invited to come to Boynton, Oklahoma—my hometown—and lead out in a community-wide night of praise. Full of anticipation at getting to share my music with the people I had grown up with, yet slightly apprehensive in knowing full well I might have to see face to face some of the people who had hurt me in the past, I prepared for the night.

I should have known that once I got there things would be fine, but once again I had allowed the subtle lies of the enemy to invade my mind to a certain degree. As I had learned by that time, though, I battled through the lies with the Truth, and faced the giants of fear and shame and past hurts with grace and favor of the Lord. The night went so well. With only about fifty people in attendance and knowing most of the people personally, the night was at once intimate and healing for me. Soaking in the triumph of having faced those giants, I was very refreshed after the concert of worship. But God had something more refreshing for me than I had bargained for.

After the concert, a little gray-haired lady, June Smith, approached me and said, "Isn't it wonderful how your grandmother Jernigan's prayers have been answered?"

Somewhat dumbfounded, I asked her what she was talking about. She said, "You don't know?"

"Don't know what?" I replied.

"Remember when you were a little boy and would go to your grandmother's house and play the piano?"

"Yes," I said. "Those are some of my most precious memories."

Going on, she asked, "And did you know she would stand behind you and pray for you?"

"How do you know that?" was all I could say.

"Every week for years, son, she would come to our weekly women's prayer meetings at church and tell us how she would ask the Lord to use you in the area of worship and music for His kingdom and for His glory...and she would ask us to agree with her in prayer. And, Dennis, we still do!" As of this writing, two of those little ladies are still alive and continue to pray for me...and I am fifty-eight years old. Grandma died when I was thirteen!

Instantly all I could think of was the list I had just made two weeks earlier, and how I had asked God to show me where He had been when my grandmother had died; why He had abandoned me in that way. Suddenly my mind was flooded with Truth as I heard Father say, "Son, you will see your grandmother again. And you thought I had forgotten you? Son, I've had you covered in prayer since day one. I multiplied your grandmother's prayers. I *never* forsook you...even for a moment."

Each memory that I had placed on that list began to come into what I call a kingdom perspective. When I was five, someone had protected me from that man's touch. All the teasing and humiliation I went through in high school was not in vain...I began to see those things as opportunities for growth rather than for being beaten down. The shame I felt due to my willful disobedience of God suddenly washed away by the Truth of God's love for me. Even the wounding at the hand of my college mentor came into a different light as I allowed Father to show me how He could take even my greatest pain and sorrow and bring from them my greatest healing and joy. And then it hit me. I would never understand nor appreciate the sweetness of the rain had I never gone through the desert episodes of my life. But He was still not through...

As Father would have it, He began to nudge me into talking with my dad about things that had happened when I was a boy, like why he could not talk with me about sex, and the biggy—why he could never verbally tell me he loved me. Because I was traveling more and more by this time, sharing my story and my music, I had the opportunity to take my dad on one of these ministry trips. Having him all to myself in my truck, I asked the Lord for grace, and I asked Daddy all the questions I had been so afraid to ask when I was younger.

"Daddy, why did you never tell me you loved me when I was growing up?" I asked, my voice shaking and my heart thumping, afraid of what he might say. But I had to know.

"Well, my dad never told me...so...I didn't know *how* to tell you."

With one simple honest question and one simple honest answer, my dad and I healed a generational wound in our family. My dad now has no trouble telling me how he feels about me. A man of few words to this day, all I needed to hear were those three little words. I would have been forever happy to have heard them only one time, having lived a lifetime without them to that point!

Another thing God began to do? Forgive those who had hurt me. I found that easier to do when I realized that *not* forgiving them was not punishing them one iota, but to not forgive them was keeping *me* locked away in the prison of my own mind. I was the only one being punished. What freedom I found in simply releasing those who had hurt me.

Yet Father was still not through. He simply said, "There's one more person you need to forgive, son."

"Who is that, Father?" I asked.

"Yourself," was all He said.

Part of my feelings of despair and depression had stemmed not only from past hurts but from how I still held myself responsible for my past choices. And, indeed, I am responsible for my choices...but I had continued punishing myself from time to time, not realizing I had received God's forgiveness but had not forgiven myself! In a sense, *my* standards were somehow higher than God's! What a liberation day it was when I simply forgave myself—and moved on.

I discovered that day that there is one thing a believer should give up all hope on. You want to know what that is? A believer should give up the hope of *ever* changing their past. It cannot be done. I discovered I had been wasting far too much of my time consumed with the "what ifs" rather than moving on into the journey God calls this life. I am not alone; never have been, never will be. He has been with me each and every step of the way on this incredible journey, and I feel as if I am just beginning.

I am who my Father says I am. My past does not define me. The gay community does not define me. The government does not define me. My feelings do not define me. My circumstances do not define me. People do not define me. Even I do not define me. Only One has that honor, and He calls me His own.

I have been utterly, irrevocably, changed...signed, sealed, delivered, a child of the King who has decided to stop sitting beneath the table of life and settling for the crumbs that fall beneath. I am a child of the King of Kings and my Father has set a table before me—in *this* life—in the midst of even my enemies and welcomes me to sit and dine fully with Him; anytime, anywhere, under any circumstances. I am His. This is my life, and it speaks for itself.

13

SELF-CONTROL

Like a city that is broken into and without walls
Is a man who has no control over his spirit.
(Proverbs 25:28)

How many times have we heard someone say something like this in reference to a recurring point of failure: "I just can't seem to help myself"? How many times have we said that very thing ourselves? That was one of my go-to mantras regarding my own failure before I became a new creation in Christ. I would fall and then repent, and then I would pledge to do better, only to fall once again and start the whole cycle anew! Another way to say it is, "Why do I keep giving in to the temptation?" We say we want to do better in regard to our temptations, yet we continue to fall. This is like being in a fortified city, only to have the walls breached because we have no self-control—like we have no choice in the matter. We may not have a choice as to the things that tempt us, but we *always* have a choice as to how we will respond. Always! Let us think about that from a kingdom point of view rather than from our own human point of view.

If we are new creations in Christ, we know that—according to God's Word—with each and every temptation, God provides a way of escape. Did you catch that? With *every* temptation, He provides a way of escape. What if your house was on fire and someone says to you, "Hey, your house is on fire! Come this way and I will help you get out!" and you respond with, "But I just can't seem to help myself! I am going to stay in this fire because I just cannot help myself!" That would be foolishness, would it not? Yet, we do the same thing with our inability to avoid giving into temptation.

Let me suggest a better way: When temptation comes—and it will—would it not be better to stop and ask the Lord, "Lord, You say that with every temptation, You will provide a way of escape. I need to see the way right now, Father. Will you show me?" It is in that simple act that some significant kingdom work is done.

In such a moment of seeking God for the way of escape, we acknowledge the reality of the temptation. In the simplest way I can explain from my personal experience, the enemy is trying to get me to focus on *me*. And where is the believer supposed to fix his eyes? On Jesus! There is power in understanding this because the power of this statement is derived from John 8:32 which tells us that Truth will set us free. My personal belief is that the first step toward Truth is our own honest confession. To own my thoughts is to step toward God in honesty. To step toward God in honesty is to let go of the thought and give it to God. In so doing, I effectively transfer ownership of the stinkin' thinkin' to Jesus. It is in that moment that I receive Truth to see the way of escape and receive the grace to head for the escape route.

Here is another practice I have incorporated into my response to temptation. Every temptation can be seen as either an encounter with the enemy or as an opportunity for intimacy with Christ. Rather than addressing the enemy, I choose to address the Father with this question: "What is it, Father?" In moments of temptation, I assume that the Lord has something for me that the enemy is trying to kill, steal, or destroy. By asking that question of Father I effectively refocus my thoughts from the enemy to the Lord. Intimacy with Christ is acknowledging the temptation but using said temptation as a catalyst to transparency with Jesus. Nothing is hidden. Shame and guilt are dealt with. I am reminded of who and whose I am. Life in Christ is used to replace death with the enemy.

The way of escape for me is as simple as turning my point of view from negative to positive by practically looking for ways to take my eyes off of *me*. Not only do I focus on intimacy with the Lord, but I begin looking for godly intimacy with others in a practical way. When I am down or depressed, I look for someone in need of encouragement. In that simple act of acknowledging the needs of another, my eyes are focused away from me and are fixed on Jesus and the needs of another. And the most amazing thing happens: my need for encouragement is met supernaturally! Could it be that this was exactly what the enemy was trying to thwart with the initial temptation? When I am sad, I look for someone to comfort. When I am financially needy, I look for someone to bless with some sort of provision. When I am confused, I look for someone who needs peace in their life and take steps to help guide them to peace. You get the idea. Meet the needs of others who face the very things you face, and Jesus will meet you both there in the moment, providing for the needs of those you bless and providing the way of escape for you. Just get your eyes off of *you*!

> *Now for this very reason also, applying all diligence, in your faith supply moral excellence, and in your moral excellence, knowledge, and in your knowledge, self-control, and in your self-control, perseverance, and in your perseverance, godliness, and in your godliness, brotherly kindness, and in your brotherly kindness, love. (2 Peter 1:5-7)*

Where does faith come into the mix? At every step of the journey! We know according to Hebrews 11:1 that "faith is the assurance of things hoped for, the conviction of things not seen." What I have come to realize is that this is the most simple of definitions, but that simplicity is packed with the power of the resurrection. With our faith in Christ, we are to walk in that faith with diligence. Diligence is persistent work or effort. We are to work at our faith persistently. We are to be stubborn in our faith, not allowing distractions to sway us from its path.

In addition to walking diligently, we are to apply moral excellence to our faith. Moral excellence is simply born out of our new nature. It is who we are. We *are* morally excellent. We just need to learn to release it. Moral excellence is thinking virtuous thoughts. This is one more aspect of renewing the mind. In our old life, our natural way of thinking was toward the un-virtuous. When we were born again, our ability to think virtuously was granted. It is up to us to put off the un-virtuous thoughts and replace them with virtuous. Replace the profane with the holy.

To our moral excellence, we are to add knowledge. The knowledge the Word is speaking of here is to renew one's mind with an ever-deepening knowledge of Christ. As always, the battle will be for your thoughts, and this is why you must decide where your worldview derives from. Do you require worldly/human-centered knowledge, or do you require God/Christ-centered knowledge to inform your identity and way of thinking? One leads to falling to temptation while the other leads to victory.

Here is where the Word of God gets very exciting for me in regard to walking in faith and in overcoming temptation. God's Word tells us to add to our knowledge of God the willful act of self-control. He would not tell us to do so were it not possible. Self-control is mastering one's own desires and sensual appetites. Let me blow your mind a bit here. The key to mastering my own desires is found in Psalm 37:4 which encourages us as follows:

Delight yourself in the LORD;
And He will give you the desires of your heart. (Psalm 37:4)

The best way I have found to master my own desires and sensual appetites is to simply delight myself in the Lord through intimate worship. To worship God requires my entire being. To worship God requires my thoughts. It requires my physical body. It requires my emotions. It helps me get my eyes off of me—the real issue here—and to get them on Jesus! In so doing, I discover my truest, deepest, most core desires are met…in *Him*! Self-control begins and ends with Jesus.

The good news is that there is even more at our disposal in walking in self-control. God's Word tells us to add something to our self-control. We are to add to it perseverance. Perseverance is patiently continuing to walk in intimacy with Christ regardless of one's circumstances. The world around us may fall apart, but He never changes. It is through perseverance—patiently continuing with God no matter what—that self-control is combined with God's grace to keep walking through the storm.

Isn't this amazing? The Word of God is a treasure trove of Truth that sets us free! In addition to adding perseverance to our self-control, we are to add godliness. Godliness is two-fold. It is the act of acknowledging God as God no matter what, and it is walking in the realization that we are His new creations. His children. Walking in godliness is simply walking in the reality of who and whose we are.

But we are not done yet. To our godliness we are to add brotherly kindness. Quite simply, brotherly kindness is regarding others with the same regard we hope to receive...even if we never receive it in return. What led me to personal repentance from stinkin' thinkin' in the first place was the kindness of the Lord and the kindness of others. To walk in brotherly kindness is to simply—yet again—walk in the reality of who and whose we are.

Last but not least, to our brotherly kindness we are to add love. The Word for love in this passage is the Greek word, *agape.* It is the same word used in John 3:16 which tells us that God so loved the world that He gave us His only Son! This kind of love is the kind that lays down its life for another. Again, this means self-control involves getting our eyes off of ourselves and placing them on the needs of others.

Self-control is getting my focus off of *me* and placing my focus on God and others. To do so means my mind—the battleground, the walled city—will walk in wholeness and protection. It does not mean we will not be bombarded with stinkin' thinkin'. It does mean that we can walk in power and victory no matter what! Self-control is part of who you are as a new creation. Believe and receive it...and walk boldly in it!

14

WORTH FIGHTING FOR

W hen I think of the lies the enemy has used to gain power over me in the past, one of the biggest is that I am not worth fighting for. There are far too many instances the liar used against me to enumerate here, but I will share a couple to illustrate how believing lies and relying on feelings is a deathtrap for the mind.

When I was a boy, I felt such constant humiliation at the realization as to how different I was from other boys. My confusion led me to conclude I was somehow something less than a real boy, so I would never put my hands in my pockets as boys and men do—because I felt I did not deserve it. It was during junior high during the onslaught of puberty that I was already entrenched in sexual sin with other boys. By this time, humiliation was a constant companion because there were several older boys who seemed determined to remind me how much of a fag and queer I was. Imagine my conflict when one of those very public antagonists was one who had just had sex with me the night before!

Due to my fear at the very public attack, and out of sheer shock at the audacity of this one who had used me being a part of the attack, I dared not risk further humiliation by outing him. This one I had trusted with my body now threatened harm. My mind was raging like an out-of-control storm in that moment, being dashed about on the rocks of fear and self-loathing and anger and shame. When all had settled down and I could begin to try and gather my thoughts, those thoughts coalesced to one thought: Dennis Jernigan is not worth fighting for. I will admit, this is one of the major schemes of the enemy against me. Who would have thought he would still be able to get this one through the filter of the Word in my mind, yet he occasionally still does. My remedy? Put off the lie and put on the Truth: Jesus Christ thought I was worth dying for!

Many years ago, I was invited to speak to a state legislature regarding same-sex marriage. Knowing the opposition I would surely face from both the gay community and the very biased media, I did not want to go alone. The thought of what I could possibly face gave me several sleepless nights and a constant gnawing in the pit of my stomach. The "what ifs" left my mind reeling and confused. Since the group that was bringing me in would pay for two people to attend, I saw this as the Lord's provision for someone strong to stand with me physically as I spoke.

Melinda was not able to go with me as someone needed to stay home with our nine children…and quite honestly, the thought of both of us being harmed in some way and leaving our children without parents took Melinda off the table as an option for a traveling companion. Naturally, I went to the leadership of my church to ask if anyone could possibly go with me. My feelings were those of hope and elation as I thought about how one of my brothers with whom I had been fighting side by side with for years would certainly be willing to stand with me in my time of need—be willing to stand for the King and for the kingdom.

Imagine the chaos in my mind as man after man turned me down. One had family obligations. One had ministry obligations. Another had work obligations. Several just did not want to get involved. In each case, I understood…to a point. In my mind, I would have laid down my life for any one of those men and their families. Yet not one would stand with me. My thoughts became even more erratic as they careened from one side of my brain to the other. The place I allowed that thought to light? *I was not worth fighting for.* When all was said and done, my brave fifteen-year-old son, Israel David, said, "I will go with you, Dad."

Reality was that, regardless of the reasons these men had given, God had ordained that my son experience this part of my life with me.

Truth overcame the lie when I realized that my son was ready, willing, and able to stand with me. Truth was, those men were not ordained for that moment in time to make that journey with me. Truth gave both Israel and me grace to walk through the protesters; to go through the mocking tones of the interviewer during the brief press conference I was afforded; to face the threatening glares of those opposed to the Truth of God's Word; and ultimate Truth was that God had triumphed over fear in my heart and had caused my son to grow in faith and grace as a result...and me too.

Going through such circumstances causes me to consider ultimate Truth. God is God. I am not. He is in control and desires nothing but my best. He allows me to—calls me to—face fire and to suffer for the sake of the gospel. There are times when a man is called to stand alone, just as Daniel did when he was thrown to the lions; just as David did when he faced Goliath; just as Jesus did when He bore the cross. We often think about the death and physical danger these men faced, but we need to remind ourselves of the rest of the story in each episode. Daniel was delivered. Goliath was defeated. Jesus rose again! Truth is that even when facing death, Dennis Jernigan is worth fighting for. Even if death should come, my eternal life was secured on the cross. For God so loved Dennis Jernigan that He gave His only Son. That is how much I am worth! I am worth His life.

If God values me that much, what does that say about how much I value myself? I am not talking about self-focus or vanity nor am I expressing narcissism. If my Maker thinks I am of great worth, should I not place as much value upon myself? My point is simple. The way in which I think about myself tells God and others what I think of God! How dare I belittle His creativity by putting myself down? How dare I devalue someone God saw as worth dying for? How dare I pridefully suggest my reasoning abilities are superior to the reason of my Creator? Dennis Jernigan does not get to call or see himself as something less than God calls him or the way He sees him.

The battleground truly is our mind. So we need to decide if our mind—our thoughts—are worth fighting for. What is worth fighting for? Would you fight for your wife's safety or for the well-being of your children? Of course—because they are worth fighting for! Would you fight for your marriage? Of course—because you know your marriage is worth fighting for! What about Truth? Is Truth worth fighting for? Let us make it more personal by getting down to the basic reality of our existence. What about your own mind? Is your mind worth fighting for?

I will be honest with you: the battle for my thoughts has been a slaughtering field at times. Sacred thoughts I held as my identity were laid waste, leaving me feeling naked and alone. At other times, the battle has left my mind absolutely numb as my overthinking gave way to simple thinking on what God calls Truth. There have been times when my mental battles have left those around me feeling bloodied and beaten along with me. But one thing I can say with absolute certainty is this: the battle has been worth every moment of sorrow and suffering and pain and humiliation along the way. Knowing Jesus intimately is worth it. I am worth fighting for...to me.

What is not worth fighting for? My opinions are not worth fighting for or losing sleep over; they are trivial matters that have no bearing on my eternal existence. What others think of me no longer has a bearing on who I am as they once did. While I am glad when others are pleased with me, what they think about me does not ultimately matter to who I am in the core of my being. Even what others do to me cannot alter who I am. I am no one's victim. I am a victor. Who and whose I am causes me to walk in both humility and in forgiveness. Jesus forgave those who crucified Him while He was in the very midst of that crucifixion! I can do no less because of who and whose I am. This fact alone saves me so much mental anguish and despair.

If I am worth fighting for to God, should I not fight for my own being? For my own thoughts? Here's what God's Word has to say about it:

> *Watch over your heart with all diligence,*
> *For from it flow the springs of life. (Proverbs 4:23)*

In this most wise Proverb, heart equals mind or innermost being. Core identity. The way you think. Part of one's fight is in building up protections for when the onslaught comes against your mind. And do not kid yourself: as long as you live on this planet, you will face the lies of the enemy. Might as well fight by the way you prepare and guard over your thought-life. God tells us to guard over our thoughts with *all* diligence because the essence of our life and existence flows from those thoughts. Get drastic! Get militant with guarding over your thoughts… and watch life begin to flow massively.

When I was first set free, one of the first things I did was to rid my life of any attachments to my past. At first, this caused my heart great anxiety and fear as I realized I was cutting loose from things I had held on to for sanity and self-worth—things that truly and honestly were counterfeits to the very things I desired! I rid my life of gifts that had been given to me. I burned letters and mementos and anything physical that could be burned. My thought was to cut off any hope of having that thing restored to me in any way. Burning seemed very logical to me! I stopped going to places I used to frequent in my old identity… and I cut off relationships that caused me to think wrong thoughts. In other words, I severed anything that tied my soul to my former identity as much as possible.

At first, this caused me much pain and sorrow, but that pain was replaced by healing and the sorrow gave way to the comfort of the Lord. Replacing what was counterfeit with what was real was a major step in setting myself up for success rather than failure. Extreme? You betcha! But my sanity has been worth it. As I have already said, my desire to know and to be known by God led me to shut off all other voices as much as possible that kept me from hearing God. I fasted from secular music and TV from 1981 until 1993. Twelve years of safety for my mind! Was it worth it? Absolutely!

How will you guard over your thoughts? Here are some practical ways I guard over mine to this day:

- Read and put on God's Word. I memorize it and its concepts.

- Talk to God—often. Invite Him into every aspect of my life.

- Listen to only the music that builds me up spiritually and morally. What we put in our mind is what we get back from our mind. Put in good things!

- Fast from certain things from time to time. Food. Drink. Places. People. TV.

- Take time to quiet my thoughts.

- As I go to sleep, I meditate on God's Word. He gives to His beloved even in their sleep (Psalm 127:2).
- Worship God daily.
- Practice gratitude.
- Ask the Lord what to wear; what to eat; what to watch; what to listen to.
- Laugh.
- Spend time with people—even if you are an introvert like me!
- Spend time with people who love me enough to speak Truth to me. Be honest with people I trust and allow them to be honest with me.
- Be about the Lord's business: serve and meet the needs of people around me. It's not about me!
- Remind myself of who and whose I am—often.
- Work at the important relationships in my life: God, spouse, children, friends, body of Christ.
- Laugh—often!

Remember to guard over your mind with all diligence because your life flows from the thoughts you think. When in doubt, I have a couple of go-to passages of scripture to help me calm my thoughts:

> "YOU SHALL LOVE THE LORD YOUR GOD WITH ALL YOUR HEART, AND WITH ALL YOUR SOUL, AND WITH ALL YOUR STRENGTH, AND WITH ALL YOUR MIND; AND YOUR NEIGHBOR AS YOURSELF." —Jesus (Luke 10:27)

Do my thoughts glorify God? Do my thoughts cause me to love people? Do my thoughts cause me to see myself as God sees me? If the answer to any one of these questions is "no," I immediately begin to ask the Holy Spirit to help me recognize the lie I am believing and to replace it with the Truth. You can do this!

> The name of the LORD is a strong tower;
> The righteous runs into it and is safe. (Proverbs 18:10)

When I feel bombarded in thought, I guard over my thoughts/ heart by reminding my soul of who God is. Like a mighty fortress of whose and who I am, I speak His names and His character to my mind, and lies are thwarted and Truth prevails. You can do this…because your mind—who you are—is worth fighting for.

15

ORIENTATION DOES NOT AN IDENTITY MAKE

Orientation is "the ability to locate oneself in one's environment with reference to time, place, and people; the ascertainment of one's true position, as in a novel situation, with respect to attitudes, judgments, etc."[5]

When one finds one's self lost in the physical world, we are really saying we are not familiar with the environment, so we do not know where we are in relation to our surroundings. We must then do what? Orient ourselves—or *re*-orient ourselves. We think nothing of reorientation in this sense…but when it comes to our identity, it's a whole new ballgame. In my own life, I once felt oriented to homosexuality but felt lost in that identity. So what did I do? I decided that I would re-orient myself.

We hear so much these days about a person's sexual orientation— as if that is what defines us. If that were the case in my life, I would be defined as a homosexual, fearful, self-focused, raging lunatic…but none of those things defines me—even if I was oriented toward them. When I was a boy, I had a temper. At the smallest of perceived threat

---

5.   http://dictionary.reference.com/browse/orientation

or perceived humiliation I would typically fly into a rage of an angry outburst, lashing out at whoever happened to be in my path. If I did not get my way, I would turn red and shake with anger. My orientation was toward anger. My mom's explanation—even when I was a boy—was that I came by it naturally. She told me on more than one occasion that my anger was in my blood due to my fiery red-headed great-grandparents. In no uncertain terms she was telling me this was my orientation.

As I grew older, I became intensely fearful of being rejected and made it a practice to go out of my way to ensure that people would like me; that I would be the best at everything so everyone would think highly of me. I was oriented to perform for the approval and acceptance of others, yet that approval-seeking orientation did not—and does not—define me.

During my entire childhood and well beyond my college years, I was oriented to being self-serving, self-seeking, and self-focused. Everything I did and portrayed myself to be was centered around me—me and my wants and desires, often at the expense of others. This was my orientation, yet I am not defined as a self-centered person any longer.

Jesus Christ gave me a brand new identity and, in the process of my relationship with Him, showed me that I am not to be defined by my past failures, by my present circumstances, by whatever may tempt me, nor by the gay community. Only One gets to define me: my Maker. When I determined that God would be the one to define me, He quickly reminded me that my original orientation was toward sin…and my particular sin was the behavior of homosexuality—even if that orientation was not by my choice. You see, we do not get to choose what will tempt us, but in Jesus I have been given the grace to choose what is holy and righteous. Orientation does not define me. Never has; never will.

My story is my story, and my story is meant to condemn no other person, yet many call me a hater for saying I used to be gay but am no more…while applauding a man who says he is a woman trapped in a man's body…while applauding anyone who comes out as gay. I'm not telling anyone they have to do anything. This is just my story…yet I am constantly condemned for coming out as straight! Who exactly is the hater? Just sayin'. I condemn no one, but God's Word is clear when it comes to what He thinks of homosexual behavior. Here are just a few of the many verses in scripture:

Do not practice homosexuality; it is a detestable sin. (Leviticus 18:22 NLT)

If a man has sex with a man as one does with a woman, both of them have done what is abhorrent. (Leviticus 20:13 TM)

They traded the truth about God for a lie. So they worshiped and served the things God created instead of the Creator himself, who is worthy of eternal praise! Amen. That is why God abandoned them to their shameful desires. Even the women turned against the natural way to have sex and instead indulged in sex with each other. And the men, instead of having normal sexual relations with women, burned with lust for each other. Men did shameful things with other men, and as a result of this sin, they suffered within themselves the penalty they deserved. (Romans 1:25-27 NLT)

As a friend once told me, we can have comfort or we can have Truth. Only Truth sets us free. God's Truth—not man's truth. God does not call temptation sin. Jesus was tempted in every manner just as we are—yet without sinning! Therefore, temptation—be it homosexual or otherwise—does not equal sin. It is what we do with the temptation that determines if we sin or not. Follow the temptation: sin. Find the way of escape: no sin.

He does

For we do not have a high priest who cannot sympathize with our weaknesses, but One who has been tempted in all things as we are, yet without sin. (Hebrews 4:15)

This means that temptation does not define us. This also means that, since we were all born oriented to sin—that orientation does not define us either. That's great news! That means if you are oriented to lying or stealing or slandering or harming others or alcohol or drugs or (you fill in the blank with whatever you're oriented toward), that you have been given a way out.

No temptation has overtaken you but such as is common to man; and God is faithful, who will not allow you to be tempted beyond what you are able, but with the temptation will provide the way of escape also, so that you will be able to endure it. (1 Corinthians 10:13)

Did you get that? God will not allow us to be tempted beyond what we are able to bear, but makes a way of escape—always. But that way of escape comes via a relationship with Him. After the Lord set me free and gave me a brand new identity, the temptation did not suddenly cease in my life. If anything it intensified…but I began to take God at His word and began to (still do) call out to Him whenever temptation would rear its ugly head. He began to remind me to respond out of my new creation nature and to see life from a new point of view: *His* point of view.

Therefore I urge you, brethren, by the mercies of God, to present your bodies a living and holy sacrifice, acceptable to God, which is your spiritual service of worship. And do not be conformed to this world, but be transformed by the renewing of your mind, so that you may prove what the will of God is, that which is good and acceptable and perfect. (Romans 12:1-2)

I was born oriented to sin. True. But that orientation no longer defines me. Just like Lazarus, I walked out of my old dead life as alive as I could be in Jesus, but I was not as free as I was going to be. Jesus told those around the risen Lazarus to loose the grave-clothes from him. He had been bound up in the bindings of death. I did not want to be merely alive. I wanted to be free from my old orientations and from my old ways of thinking, and through a relationship with Jesus Christ, I was set free (and still in process!). Are you tired of being defined by your orientation or by your temptations? You can be free. Free to be who Father God has called you to be all along. Jesus Christ will meet you and love you right where you are…but the best news of all is that He loves you enough to not leave you there. Seek Jesus for the answers you need.

16

IN FEELINGS OR TRUTH WE TRUST

When I was born again...

What changes when we are born again? Our old self dies by faith—and our new self is raised to life in Christ Jesus by faith. Being born again is being brought to life and set upon an incredible journey of discovery. Being born again is the beginning of the most grand adventure that provides the traveler with the most mesmerizing vistas the mind of man could never conceive apart from God! On this journey I have discovered never-ending mountains of His healing, fathomless oceans, and wave upon wave of His love. Forest upon magnificent forest of all manner of life His Truth provides! Every day is a brand new opportunity to explore what it means to be born again. Just take the next step—and be prepared to have your mind blown!

If you are feeling (there's that pesky word again!) like your life is at a standstill, just take the next step. You never get to your destination unless you take the first—or next—step. Perhaps your current situation and circumstances make you feel like you are living in hell on earth. As Winston Churchill supposedly so famously said, "If you're going through hell, keep going." Even those feelings of "hell on earth" are as the result of a thought you are mulling over in your mind. What do we do in such moments? We change our point of view by asking the Lord to show us our hell from His perspective! When we have ascertained that, we put off the wrong thought and exchange it for the right thought… and we do that until the right thinking becomes the overcoming thinking.

The following are some tips and things you will need for the trip:

1. **Map, GPS, personal guide, and roadside assistance, all in one**: You will need a guide for your journey—and I have the most wonderful news! The Lord has given us the Holy Spirit to guide us through our spiritual journey. He is better than OnStar! He is always with us. Never sleeps. Never takes a break. We have but to acknowledge Him and He is ready and willing to meet whatever need we have! Walking in the power and filling of the Holy Spirit is like having the world's best GPS and best roadside assistance possible. He is available day and night, twenty-four/seven. We have but to decide if we will trust Him or trust our feelings. He will never contradict the Word, while feelings often do!

2. **Know your final destination**: When taking a journey, we generally have a destination in mind. Our destination? Wholeness in Jesus. How do we get there? We seek Jesus and we follow the roadmap. What is our roadmap? The Word of God. When in doubt, go to the Word!

3. **A traveling companion**: The joy of getting there is in the journey—and every journey is made sweeter and joy made more tangible when we have someone to share it with. I know it is redundant, but we are *never* alone—even if we feel like it! And what do we do when our feelings are messing with our journey? We get to the Truth. And Jesus is *the* Truth.

4. **Provisions**: Heading out on our journey, we never know what we may encounter. We may find ourselves stranded by high water or deep snow. Regardless of what tries to hinder our journey, we must have provisions along the way. And guess what? Our traveling Companion is both food and drink! Jesus is the Bread of Life. Jesus is Living Water. We but need to eat and drink of His presence whenever our soul is hungry or thirsty.

5. **Extra fuel**: From time to time, we will grow tired and weary in the journey, but, again, our Companion provides the filling of power and He even provides rest as we undertake whatever leg of the journey we find ourselves on.

Teaching, instructions

"Take My yoke upon you and learn from Me, for I am gentle and humble in heart, and YOU WILL FIND REST FOR YOUR SOULS. *For My yoke is easy and My burden is light." —Jesus (Matthew 11:29-30)*

yoke— bind together

Now may the God of hope fill you with all joy and peace in believing, so that you will abound in hope by the power of the Holy Spirit. (Romans 15:13)

6. **Keep your eyes on the road**: While that goes without saying, we need to remember one of the ploys of the enemy is to try and get us focused on the failures of our past. To live our lives according to our past failures is equivalent to driving down the road by looking in the rearview mirror. Doing so leads to nothing but disaster! We use the rearview mirror simply to glance back occasionally to help us keep our bearings. This reminds us of how far we have come and helps us stay oriented on the *Truth*!

7. **Good music**: When Melinda and I travel, we often put on the music of 2nd Chapter of Acts and Keith Green—and sing! There is nothing like worshiping Jesus and singing as if no one is listening to cover the sometimes tedious parts of the journey with sheer joy. Worship helps us maintain our focus on Truth. Truth always set us free and takes our eyes off of us. Sing your way to Truth and to freedom.

8. **Do not fear the side trips**: Life has a way of taking us down unexpected roads. Rather than dread such momentary side trips, why not turn the point of view around to put on a heart of adventure? Unexpected circumstances are simply opportunities to watch God come through! It is the little spontaneous adventures that often lead to the grandest of vistas and deepest release of joy.

115

9. **Expect grand vistas:** The first time I saw the Grand Canyon with my children took my breath away. It was so massive my human brain could not fathom what I was seeing, which made me think I was seeing a grand panoramic painting! As my children stood their mouths agape at the splendor, my heart was ravished with deep joy at sharing this unexpected splendor with those I love most. Our attitude, when traveling with the children, was to make each and every experience the children had a learning experience if possible, regardless of how mundane or non-special the landscape might appear.

When the children were younger—and still at home—we made every trip a lesson of some sort, teaching the children to look at the world from different points of view. At the ocean, we encouraged them to experience wave after wave and to imagine how these waves compared to God's love for them. In the Rocky Mountains of Colorado we encourage them to imagine seeing life from the top and to imagine life in the valley…how much you could see from the mountaintops, but how true life was lived in the valleys below. In the forests we encouraged them to see life from the grand majesty of the trees to the minuteness and diversity of life below, from fern to chipmunk and turtle to insect. Even when traveling through the monotony the flatlands of Kansas can be, we encouraged them to look for the beauty found in wide open expanses. Honestly, there was not one place we ever traveled through that we were not able to find beauty— and evidence of God's presence and power.

Walking the journey of life with Jesus is—can be—like that. It is our choice. How we live our lives depends a great deal on how we view our circumstances. Will we view them through the filter of our feelings or through the filter of what is true and real? As with our children, we need to always be looking for the best vantage point and vista, striving to get to God's point of view.

When stranded in the desert of sorrow, I choose to see and curl up into the comfort of His presence. When slogging through the tar pit of pain, I choose to see an opportunity to experience the healing of God's very near and real presence with me. When caught in the wilderness of

116

suffering, I choose to see the great cloud of witnesses—champions of the faith—who have paved the way for me. I choose to believe God's Word concerning suffering and allow the fiery trials of life to burn away all that is not of the Lord. It is from the ashes of my suffering that eternal life and love are produced…and the real me comes forth, shining like gold.

When in a storm of chaos and confusion, I choose to put off the lies that say standing for Truth is not worth it, and I replace those thoughts with thoughts of God's very presence proving peace in the very midst of that storm. As when I would take my children tornado hunting, it is an amazing and surreal moment to be in a storm, being tossed by the wind, hearing the thunder, startled at a sudden burst of lightning, yet actually enjoying the majesty of God's hand and presence.

When in a tsunami of temptation, I choose to actively ask for God to reveal the way of escape, and without fail, He lifts me by my wings of faith, buoying me up by the wind of the Spirit and Truth of His Word, allowing me to soar above that temptation as if I were an eagle ruling over the sky, experiencing His glory while the world is swept away below me.

Believer. Follower of Christ. New Creation. You are not on any simple journey. You are on the grandest adventure—a trek full of wonder and thrills and twists and turns…that lasts this life and the next. Are your ready for the journey? Put off the lies that say you can't and put on the Truth that says you can and will…and then take the next step in Truth. The feelings you long for—hope, joy, health, peace, security, destiny, purpose—will follow suit, in spite of the circumstances you find yourself in. And if you fall, just keep getting back up and heading for the Truth. It looks like Jesus!

17

IN REPAIR, BEING RESTORED

My wife, Melinda, has been through much in her own life and journey of renewing her mind. The following is what she felt led to share to help you along in your journey:

There is a Japanese tradition known as Kintsugi, or "golden repair," that uses a unique restoration technique for the repair of broken ceramics. The process begins by taking a cracked portion of pottery and mending it with a concoction of powder and precious metals such as gold, silver, and platinum. To facilitate the repair of a broken vessel, the master craftsman recognizes there is beauty hidden in the broken places. He realizes that even the imperfections tell a story that enhances the worth of the vessel, even before the process has begun. The vessel's worth is not necessarily due to the vessel's appearance, but in the object itself. Instead of trying to conceal the brokenness, the artisan brings it to the forefront!

So that piece of pottery was me. I was broken, worthless, useless, and ugly—or so I was told and ultimately began to believe. Let me explain.

I have always been an "I can make it" kind of girl. I get that attitude both from my mom and my dad. My mom taught me to sew and to use even the scraps others might throw away to create something useful, to meet a need. My dad taught me to cook without a recipe and to try almost any kind of food. He taught me how to sell anything, how to work a room, and how to entertain others. He was gregarious and outgoing, as am I. Due in part to my genetics, but due in part to my need for my father's affirmation, I tend to be the same way. I used to perform to be accepted. The difference now is that I perform because I am accepted.

My father, as most fathers might attest to, was not a perfect father. My dilemma, even as I write these words, is to honor my father in all I say or do…but I also have the need to tell my story as a means of helping someone else who finds themselves thinking as I did. What tore me down in my past, Father God has used to build me up along the way!

My experiences with my dad drove me to the place of trying to hide my hurt and to the ability to sneak behind his back so as to avoid the response to my perceived shortcomings that tended to result in the slap of his hand across my face as he lost his temper. Nothing I ever did was ever right or ever seemed good enough to please him. In such moments, I began to think terrible thoughts about myself: that women are not worth much and need to be beaten into submission…deserving only to be pushed around…verbally put down. My thoughts were that others were not as important as him. This was my example—and my first guide—to who I thought I was. His opinion was beaten into my mind—mostly by his words. If he saw me as ugly, I saw myself as ugly. If he thought I was fat, I saw myself in a similar fashion. My conclusion? I was not worth much to him; therefore, I was worthless.

The verbal abuse hurt the most, because it seemed constant, daily reminding me who my father communicated to me I was—whether intentional or not. No matter what I tried to placate him, I could not "fix" it. The gulf between my need for love and acceptance and my desire to please my father left me feeling desperate, insecure, lost, and alone. This desperation led me right down the path to overcompensation—in everything—just to find even a small glimpse of affirmation, love, gentleness, and acceptance from my dad.

As children most often do, I began to identify myself in the image my father spoke and demonstrated to me. Whenever I messed up, I tried to fix it by performing up to his unreachable standards. I was desperate, insecure, and lost. I felt so alone. I overcompensated in everything just to find even a glimpse of affirmation, love, gentleness, and acceptance from my dad. Over time, I began to cover up those cracks with my performance thinking that could fill the void. I had to be the best, the first, the loudest—to be seen and known. Wanting so badly to have acceptance and the affirmation from my father, but not always being treated with the gentleness and comfort that I so desired and deserved, resulted in my poor choices, my sin. I was performing my way through life, the good church girl, smart student, wearing a mask to hide the disgust and shame I felt. I sought out relationships with men thinking the sexual attention I received would build me up and give me confidence when in reality it just left me feeling frightened and used—alone.

Even though my dad said he loved me, he did not always speak to me or respond to me in tones or actions that expressed that love. As is often the case, hurt people hurt people. The way I thought my father perceived me, along with the lies I had believed about myself, coupled with my sin, brought with it a cycle of self-pity. Every time I had an idea or made a mistake, I put myself down instantly. The image that I had for myself was that "I wasn't good enough!" Whenever conflict came and I felt attacked, I would run away or burst into tears. My longing was that someone would see me as worth defending—worth fighting for. Because of the lies I had believed, I did not have the sword of God's Truth to protect myself, nor did I understand that my faith in Christ could be a shield for use in protecting myself. I didn't have the right tools. I had so many wounds that I didn't think that anything or anyone could fix them. I had tried and tried. My conclusion? If my dad didn't think I was worth fighting for, if perfection and performance didn't work, and sex couldn't give me what I truly needed, was there even hope?

This way of thinking was of course self-focused and deeply wounding. If my dad could only have seen how much I needed his affirmation— not his condemnation. This was my burden as a girl, and this was my burden through high school and college. Even after Dennis and I met and dated off and on through college, I graduated more confused than ever. My relationship with him had seemed so promising, yet even he had let me down. This loss of hope left me absolutely desperate. Diving right into graduate school, the pressure soon got to me and the Lord began to reveal Himself to me in a very tangible way. In His loving way, He kindly led me to realize I had been placing my hope in the wrong things. My hope is not in what my earthly father thinks of me. My hope is not in my performance. My hope is not in people or possessions. When everything was stripped away from me, I came to realize my hope was in God and in God alone. Just as Dennis was experiencing in his own life, God was working in me the very same things. Through the leadership of the Holy Spirit, we were reunited and married soon after.

Soon after Dennis and I were married, the scars had begun to heal, but the cycle of self-pity still reared up its ugly head every time we argued or I perceived he was not pleased with me or I did not measure up or do something "perfectly." Those childhood memories stayed with me and haunted my every thought and view I had for and of myself. Some of my cracks were still there, needing repair.

I remember the exact day when I had my "lightbulb" moment, my Jehovah Tsidkenu, "He is my Righteousness" enlightenment. We had amazing banners at the church we led worship at. During a time of worship, I was standing under the one that said, "I Am—Jehovah Tsidkenu—I Am Your Righteousness." The Lord was using this special time of pouring my heart out to Him and declaration of who I am while singing Dennis's song, "You Are My King":

> *You are my King*
> *You are my Righteousness*
> *You are my King*
> *You are my Holiness*
> *You are my King*
> *You are my Sanctity*
> *You are my Lord*
> *You are the God of me*

You are my reason for being
You are my King

And in that moment, I got it. I really got it! I am all of these things!
In Christ, I am holy because He is Holy! I am Righteous because He
is righteous! I am all of who He is because I am in Him. I remember
how the room felt, how it smelled, all of my senses responding as if
being renewed and awakened and heightened in every way; one of
those times when there was no doubt the Lord, by His Spirit, was
doing a work in me. But that was only the beginning of my renewal
process. The revelation was there, but now I needed tools to help me
fight against the lies and negative thought patterns.

One area that I started with was recognizing the lies I was believing
about myself. I began to lay out how words that had been spoken to
me wounded me; how they had shaped the way I thought, and how
I treated and responded to others, good or bad. Being a planner, I
use lists to help me visualize my plan for action, so I began to make
my own list or Truths to help me visualize and recognize the lies for
what they were and to replace them with the Truth of God's Word.
No longer was I without tools of restoration and repair, but I had
weapons for the spiritual battle being waged for my mind.

Confession is the first step to being free. Honest confession is me
presenting my raw and unrefined heart to Him, trusting Him to
make me into who He says I am. In that moment, who I am is like
a raw gem—like a diamond in the rough. A diamond requires many
cuts to create the prisms or facets that create its brilliance. Even after
the cutting away of the rough edges, polishing ensues. Unseen by the
naked eye, there are still flaws. Most cannot be seen without some
sort of magnification—but the jeweler, the Maker, knows they are
there—so, He keeps refining and crushing and polishing and honing
until He reaches the desired design. I can trust my Maker because
He is the Master Jeweler. He knows my heart and my intentions,
the misunderstood. He gets me when even my own family doesn't. He
loves me even when I am lonely—or I think I am. Do you filter your
thoughts, words, or speech? Do you cover up and share just the good

parts or do you really get to the root? Your answer to these questions could be the difference between victory and defeat.

So after cutting off the lies and polishing my heart, what is the Truth? Here is my list:

1. Recognize the lie, put it off, and replace it with the Truth.
2. I cannot control everything.
3. Woundings can be a good thing.
4. I don't quit.

Sin sees to it that we will be wounded in this life. What we choose to do with those woundings is the difference between life and death. Choose to speak life to your own mind. We are people of choice. Growth—living—is a process of constant restoration. Working through this restoration process won't be easy and will take time. That is okay. The intimacy and work of the Lord can leave us raw, like right after a tattoo (or what I imagine getting a tattoo might by like), and needs time to heal before the beautiful work is finished and revealed. Like the tradition of Kintsugi used to repair the broken ceramic jar, your process will be a journey of healing and the restoration of beauty. It may not look pretty in the beginning, but using the right materials and tools to bring your soul back to life will require a vulnerability that can only be handled by the Maker, the Heavenly Father—the Master Craftsman and True Artisan of your identity. And don't expect your heart to look like the original piece. Your heart will shift to make room for new life and additions made through this process. Like the once-broken vessel, you will be restored and made new. You won't look like you did when the process started, but you will be refined in all of the right places. Your imperfections will be covered by God's grace, instead of shame. Your cracks will be filled with the Truth you speak to yourself every day. I am marked eternally by the Word and the work on my heart and spirit. No one can ever take that away. It is permanent. Now, believe that for yourself. Put on the Truth and be made new.

18

THE PROCESS OF
HEALING

When faced with the need for healing of our minds—the way we think about ourselves—the enemy would love for us to feel overwhelmed by the mountainous terrain that our stinkin' thinkin' raises before us. Let us remember that we are on a journey—an adventure—here and that journeys require time and planning. After all, it may have taken years to build up the mountains of wrong thinking you now experience, so it may take years to tear it down. Like a building that we build with our thoughts, we tend to build it brick by brick. When tearing down that building, it is often necessary to tear it down in the same way: brick by brick, thought by thought. Bottom line? Healing is a process. The process of healing was brought home to me through the years in very tangible ways, complete with physical reminders of deep spiritual Truths.

Many years ago, I was working on my farm with my tractor. Having been grading the gravel road to and from my barn using the box blade scraper, I needed to take the heavy implement off so I could attach the brush hog and do some mowing. A box blade is like a small road grading blade one can attach to one's tractor and scrape dirt and gravel and the like. While the blade itself is about five feet across and twenty-four inches deep, on the front of the implement are four long spikes called rippers that are spaced in front of the blade. The rippers cut through the ground and break it up, allowing the scraper to then come along behind and scrape the broken ground up. The entire apparatus weighs several hundred pounds.

In a hurry to get to my next task, and having performed the changing of implements many times before, I did not take the time to go through all the necessary safety steps. As I disconnected the hydraulic arm to which the right side of the blade was attached to the tractor, it slipped off before I was ready—because of the vibrations of the still-running tractor. Before I could get out of the way, the blade fell from the tractor and onto my right leg. The ripper did its job, ripping right into my lower calf and pinning me in a very awkward position beneath the large rear tire of the tractor.

My first thoughts? I do not wish to die this way. The tractor was still running and the goats, notorious for climbing on any and everything, were nearby. All I could think—and I am serious about this—was my friends would mock the way I died at my funeral! "Can you believe he was killed by goats?" If I ever needed to be in control of my thoughts, it was in that moment. After serval minutes of pleading with the Lord to help me find the strength to remove myself from this entrapment, He came through. As I looked down at the wound, I saw a gaping hole in my leg exposing my tendon, muscle, and bone.

Not realizing I was in shock, I could only think of covering the wound and getting the flap of dangling flesh back in its proper place. Calmly, I pulled the flesh over the hole in my leg and held it there, walking all the way from behind the barn to the house bent over awkwardly while trying to keep the flesh in place. As I neared the house, Melinda came out and I showed her the wound. Wasting no time, she helped me get into the car, and she drove speedily to the nearest ER seven miles away. Nearing the ER, I told her to simply drop me off and park the car while I did the preliminary check-in.

Approaching the nurse station, I told the receptionist that I had injured myself and needed help. She calmly replied, "You'll need to fill out some paperwork." Still in shock, I felt overwhelmed to the point I could do no more. Turning around from the window, I simply slumped to the floor beneath the window—and sat. As Melinda came through the door, she asked, "What are you doing down there?" All I could muster to say was, "I need to do some paperwork." Bursting through the ER door to the triage unit, Melinda shouted, "My husband needs help!" And help came.

Two surgeries later, I was sent home to heal. Miraculously, there were no broken bones. Just nerve damage and the wound itself, which had been nicely stitched closed, seemed merely incidental after the fact. A lot of trauma for such a seemingly small wound. Little did I know but that little wound would have a far-reaching effect upon my life—and the way I think.

After a few days of rest and recuperation, I noticed the bruising around the wound was not getting any better. In fact, the flesh over the wound seemed to be growing darker and darker, fading from deep blue to deeper black. And it began to develop an odor—like rancid, decaying flesh. Since this did not seem right, I went back to the surgeon and showed him my wound. Without saying a word, he simply began to cut away the flesh, once again leaving a gaping hole in my lower calf, revealing the inner parts once again. I asked him, "When can you do a skin graft to cover the wound?" His answer sent holy chills through my being: "A skin graft will not work for this kind of wound. For this type of wound to heal properly, it must heal from the inside out."

With those words, "It must heal from the inside out," I knew in that moment that the Lord was going to be teaching me a few deeper things about healing. Confused, I asked him what he meant. I asked him how that could be possible. He then explained to me the process of healing. His instructions, while simple, were full of profound, life-giving Truth. He instructed me to soak the wound twice a day in a bucket of warm water. In that water, I was to mix a cup of Tide detergent and soak for thirty minutes. His explanation for this? The wound needs to be as clean as possible in order to promote healing.

As those words sank into my mind, I could not help but think of and relate this need for cleansing to the human need to confess one's sins. As I have already stated in a previous chapter, you will know the Truth and the Truth will set you free...but the first step Truth requires is our own honest confession—or cleansing! And the added bonus? Simply learning to rest in—soak in—God's presence! Awesome in and of itself, but the doctor was not through.

Following up the need for soaking and constant cleansing, he prescribed a large roll of gauze, sterile and clean. I was to pack the wound with said gauze as soon as I was through with my morning soak…packing it as tightly as possible so as to not allow any foreign materials into the wounded place. In addition, he instructed me to pull the gauze out before soaking at the end of the day. Curious, I asked him why. He told me that as I pulled the gauze out—which will probably hurt a bit, but will be worth the pain—any dead and decaying material would adhere to the gauze and be removed from the wound, bringing even more cleansing. Awesome! But wait, there was more!

"As you remove the gauze, make the edges of the wound bleed as much as possible." What? His words once again sent chills through my soul. "There is life in the blood. The blood will bring life-giving nutrients to the wounded places, and slowly but surely, the wound will gradually close as the flesh grows back." All I heard was, "There is life in the blood." Just as with the physical nature of the healing properties of my physical blood, the life of a new creation is healed as the blood of Jesus—the cleansing, redeeming, healing, mind-changing, debt-paying blood of Jesus—is applied to the wounds of our mind by simple faith!

As time went by, my mind was consumed with such thoughts. As my mind began to heal in new ways, so the wound on my leg began to heal. Pondering this process, I understood the need for cleansing. With honest confession comes Truth. Truth sets me free. As I placed my faith in the power of the blood of Jesus Christ, the wounded places in my mind began to come back into spiritual alignment with God's Truth.

Confession and the blood were easy to see, but I still did not fully understand the need for packing the wound. So I asked the Lord what the packing material for my spiritual, mental wounds was. He simply whispered to my mind, "Son, what did you pack into your wound that came as a result of leaving your past identity?"

Without missing a beat, I said to Him, "What shall we say, then? Am I to continue in sin so that grace may increase? May it never be! How shall I who died to sin still live in it?" That's Romans 6:1-2.

Before I could say another word, He asked, "And what did you pack in the wounded place when the enemy would threaten you with humiliation and condemnation?" Again, without hesitation, I quoted Micah:

Do not rejoice over me, O my enemy. Though I fall I will rise; Though I dwell in darkness, the LORD is a light for me. (Micah 7:8)

And then it hit me. The packing material of my life since being born again had been the Word of God! In every wounded place caused by the lies of the enemy, I had packed the Word of God, and just as with that physical gauze, I would pull the Word out of the wound and drag out more impurities. Then I would repack the wound again and again and again! Healing is a process—and I thought the lessons I had learned from the tractor incident were it…but there was still more.

After a year of healing in my body and in my mind, I was finally well enough to play basketball again. In my first pickup game since my wounding, I was making a cut toward the basket—when someone hit me on the back of my left ankle with what felt like a baseball bat! Sounding like a literal explosion in my mind, the piercing pain sent me spinning around, crumpled, to the floor. Writhing in pain, I shouted to my buddies, "Who hit me? Did you guys see who hit me?"

Confused at my response, one of the guys simply said, "DJ, there was no one near you. No one hit you."

The MIR later that evening revealed a completely shattered and severed Achilles tendon. Due to the circumstances, we had to wait ten days for the surgery to take place. As soon as I came out from under anesthesia, the surgeon said, "Mr. Jernigan, we did not have enough of your tendon left to put you back together."

Before he could continue, I moaned, "Oh, no!" in disappointment.

Continuing, he simply said, "But we were able to repair the tear."

"But, how?" I asked.

"During the time between the wounding and the surgery, so much scar tissue had formed that we were actually able to harvest some of that material and bridge the gap between the wounded places. We put you back together."

By whose scars and wounds and own torn flesh was I granted healing that bridged the gap between my wounded, broken places and the Maker of the Universe? By the scars of Jesus I am being healed! Healing is a process...and scars are like altars testifying to the healing power of God! What do my scars represent?

When I was a small boy, I was in the pasture petting one of our horses. We called him Big Red. As I petted him, he began to nip at my fingers. This caused great fear in my little heart. Spying the mulberry tree on the fence line, I ran with all my might to the safety of the tree as Big Red kept pace with my little-boy run for my life!

Safely climbing the tree to what I thought would be refuge, I was horrified to realize that Big Red could still reach me! My only recourse? I could jump the barbed wire fence to the safety and security of the other side! If there had been an Olympic event called *fence straddling*, I would have won gold that day.

No sooner had I been released from the ER than my mom asked me how I was doing. My response? "I can't wait to show the scar to my brothers and my cousins!"

A scar is what's left of a wound as a reminder that says—in a spiritual sense—"Yes, I went through that terrible, horrible, hurtful event...but look what my God did!" That is a kingdom-of-God perspective on the process of healing. Own your scars, but give glory to God. Rather than those hurtful memories being like stones draped around your neck that drag you down to despair and self-focus, cut them away with the Truth that says, "Yes, I went through that, but see what my God has done!" Healing is a process—a process meant to restore hope and bring healing at every point along the journey. Even when pain is involved, joy can be the result if the process is seen from the Maker's point of view. Who made doctors? Who gave man the wisdom to create medicine? Who is the ultimate Healer? The One who made us.

One more thing. There is only one time a follower of and believer in Christ should give up hope. We should give up the hope of ever changing our past! Stop trying! It cannot be done. Face it in honest confession and go through the process of healing in the areas of past failure and regret. Allow the Lord to take the rabble and messes of your life and bring something beautiful out of the rabble and the mess! He is able if we let

Him see our wounded places. Open up your heart to Him and let Him be the Great Physician. He is a safe place for healing to take place. Soak in His presence. Pack the Word into the wounds of your mind. Apply the healing balm of His cleansing blood to your wounds and allow His own wounding to bridge the gap between you and your Maker.

My final thought: I am healed. I am being healed. I will be healed. Where I am is in process...and the process looks a lot like Jesus!

19

The Wreckage of Resentment

If you are breathing, you have been hurt by someone else in some way or another. Those hurts tend to pile up in our minds. So, what do we do with those piled up hurts? We must forgive and move on. Easier said than done, but remember where the battleground is. The battle is in our mind, and bitterness—resentment, unforgiveness—must be dealt with in order to live the healthiest mental life possible.

While meditating on what forgiveness means and what the benefits of forgiveness are to the human soul, I asked the Lord to give me an analogy that would help me understand the power of forgiveness in a very personal way. As I got into my car and headed for town to run some errands, this picture came.

What if...while driving to town, I came to a red light and waited for the light to change? Once the signal turned green, I proceeded into the intersection only to be t-boned by a speeding vehicle. Once the gnarled vehicles came to a stop and the dust began to clear, I realized that I had been severely wounded. I could not move either leg. My arms seemed to be broken and I had experienced very obvious head and internal injuries; yet, I was wide awake and very ultra-aware of my surroundings.

Looking over to the other vehicle now enmeshed with my own, I saw the other driver calmly get out of his car and, obviously intoxicated, walk away without so much as even a scratch! As emergency personnel began to surround me and begin the extrication process, I became incredulous. "Why did he do that? Somebody stop him! He's getting away! That man did this! Get him!"

But nobody seemed to be listening. Their only intent was in getting me out of that crushed car and getting me the help I needed. But there was a problem. Once they had freed my compacted legs, I refused to let go of the wreckage. "I am not leaving this car until that man pays for what he did!" Confused, the EMTs tried in vain to get me to understand that they could not help me if I would not let go of the wreckage.

As they pleaded with me to trust them, I became ultra-focused on the one who had injured me and not on my need to let go. The EMTs explained very clearly that if I would just let go, they could get me to a very competent surgeon whose specialty was dealing with my particular injuries. In fact, they went on, this physician was the greatest in the world, and he was a short ambulance ride away…if I would only let go. Yet I would not let go.

Having no other recourse, the EMTs and the police had no other choice but to leave me there in my misery and go about their jobs of rescuing those who were willing to leave the wreckage of their lives behind and get help. Pushing my wreckage to the side of the road, seasons passed and months gave way to years, but I kept hanging on to that wreckage because the one that did this to me must pay!

Eventually, I simply learned how to move the wreckage wherever I went, often asking others to help me drag the wreckage along. Somehow, changing the location of the wreckage made it seem better for a while. But the reality was that even though I had changed my location and was feeling some relief, the injuries had never gotten the chance to heal because I was unwilling to leave the wreckage behind and go to the doctor for help. I could say it like this: "Oh, my marriage is hurting…just put me in another marriage and I will be fine"—but all I've really done is to carry this stuff into other locations, thinking that will heal me, while the truth is I carry it with me without the possibility of healing. In fact, I've moved my wreckage around so much that I don't even remember or know the root of my issues anymore because I have carried it so long. I believe, incorrectly, that I have a current issue—when the truth is that a longstanding issue is the reality. I just refuse to look at it.

The reality was that the one who had hurt me had gone on with his life. Reality was that I had made the choice to stay with the wreckage rather than go on to healing...but everyone knew I was hurt because it was obvious to everyone who passed by. I was the victim. I was the hurt one. Didn't anyone care?

Such a story would sound like foolishness if it were to happen in real life, wouldn't it? Yet, the reality is that most of us live that way in relation to our ability to forgive others. Unforgiveness—resentment—is like that. Being unwilling to forgive those who hurt us is like staying with the wreckage after a bad accident. As long as we hang on to that resentment, we cannot receive the healing that the Great Physician offers. So how do we get there?

What exactly does forgiveness mean? Quite simply, it means to release. Unforgiveness, or resentment, means to rethink or to hold on to. As my friend, Pastor Alex Himaya says, "Unforgiveness leaves you stuck in neutral." How true! As long as we remain stuck in our resentment, it's like trying to get somewhere in a car that remains in neutral. Unforgiveness gets us absolutely nowhere but deeper in despair. As the 2009 movie "Medea Goes to Jail" so eloquently and humorously puts it, "forgiveness is not for the one that hurt you; it's for you!"

There have been so many times in my life in which I have been deeply hurt. A year ago I was hurt by someone I trusted deeply, resulting in a depth of hurt that sent me reeling for several months. Saying I forgave them and actually forgiving them were two entirely different matters! I did not want to forgive because the truth was I wanted them to pay for what they had done. Guess what happened? I began to have health issues that I could not attribute to anything but stress. And guess what I could trace most of my stress back to? That's right. Resentment. Unforgiveness. Not letting go and going on.

After a while, I began to listen to the promptings of the Lord and awakened to what I had been doing. I would never move on unless I let go of the wreckage. I could never receive healing as long as I remained at the debris pile. I could never move on to what God had for me as long as I chose to live in the ruins. Unforgiveness is nothing more than holding someone else in bondage in our hearts as a way to hurt them. The only problem with that is that we are only hurting ourselves and those we are in relationship with. Once I saw what I was doing, I came to the realization that I had only one option. I must forgive.

While sitting under the teaching of Alex Himaya recently, my wife and I were very blessed to hear his thoughts on the subject of forgiveness. The next four points were gleaned from what I learned from him. If forgiveness is so good for us, what exactly are the benefits of forgiveness?

1. Emotional Benefit

Resentment kills a fool, and envy slays the simple. (Job 5:2 NIV)

Remember, resentment simply means to rethink an old hurt. When we constantly rethink an offense toward us, we continue to be enslaved to that person and that offense. We are the constant victim and never get to the place of victory. Is that really where life is? Is that really where we want to live—always the whiner? Always the victim? Not I! As Job so eloquently put it, "Resentment kills a fool!" When we are constantly reliving the old offenses, we naturally come to a place where we become numb emotionally. In the most real sense, that is when we are truly controlled by our emotions and held captive there by our stubborn refusal to let the other person go. I discovered that my ability to *feel* alive had drastically diminished due to my inability to truly forgive and let the offending party go. Once I let go, life and my ability to feel again rushed in! Over the past few weeks of truly forgiving, I have been flooded with insight and music and creativity in general. It's as if a dam had been broken in my heart. What a benefit!

2. Relational Benefit

Be kind and compassionate to one another, forgiving each other, just as in Christ God forgave you. (Ephesians 4:32 NIV)

When did Jesus forgive us? Before we ever sinned! What was the cross all about? In a very real way, Jesus practiced preemptive forgiveness. What a way to live! He forgave us before we ever existed, and He knew we would reject Him! If I truly want to live the most abundant life possible, I must be prepared to forgive before the offenses of life ever occur. I know that sounds crazy, but it is a scriptural principle. I do not plan to sin, but I do have a plan of attack when temptation comes. I immediately begin looking for the way of escape, because Jesus promised me He would have one for me. When I am hurt and tempted to be unforgiving, I need to be looking for the way of escape.

If you think about it, when we forgive someone we give them a gift by letting them go. And we give ourselves a gift by letting them go because this releases us to get the healing we need for the very real hurt we have experienced. Unforgiveness actually binds you to those you don't forgive, while forgiveness removes the last connection between you and the offense and frees you to move on with your life. Unforgiveness is like being on a treadmill: resentment takes you absolutely nowhere.

One of the ways I know if I have not forgiven someone is if I constantly bring up the same old list of hurts whenever I think of them. If you have a mental offense list that you constantly default to, you have not forgiven. You are still on that treadmill that goes nowhere.

So, just how did Jesus prepare us to respond preemptively? Let's look at the Word of God:

Then Peter came to Jesus and asked, "Lord, how many times shall I forgive my brother or sister who sins against me? Up to seven times?"

Jesus answered, "I tell you, not seven times, but seventy-seven times." (Matthew 18:21-22 NIV)

This was not meant to be *the* numerical standard of how many times we should forgive. I believe it was meant to be our attitude—that we are to forgive as many times as necessary. To me it means that I need to be prepared to forgive in an instant. Forgiving someone who has offended you puts the ball back in their court and relieves your burdened soul. Forgiveness does not lessen the hurt but it does hasten healing.

When we do not forgive, we effectively dam up our own hearts. Even if no one else can see the resentment, it is still there affecting our ability to relate to others in a healthy way. When we have a blockage in our physical heart, no one can necessarily see it, but every part of our body is affected because the heart's ability to pump life-giving blood is lessened. We may not see the lack of flow right away, but it is there. If we want full flowing relational life, we must forgive.

3. Physical Benefit

A heart at peace gives life to the body, but envy [resentment] rots the bones. (Proverbs 14:30 NIV)

A study recently conducted at Stanford University discovered what God's Word has been saying all along: unforgiveness causes physical ailments. This study revealed that resentment and envy are toxic to the body and that forgiving those who have offended you can cut stress by 50 percent. In addition, another study showed that women who had struggled with drug dependency and subsequent relapse were drastically less likely to fall back into drug use when forgiveness was practiced.

Personally I can vouch for my own study. The more I forgive and go on with my life, the less stress I have. The less stress I carry around, the more joy and contentment I feel in my life. The more joy and contentment I walk in, the less likely I am to fall into temptation. The more I let go, the more freedom I have in relating in a healthy, productive way to my wife, my children, my friends, and all those I minister to. Forgiveness really is one of the keys to abundant life.

4. Spiritual Benefit

Jesus lived a lifestyle of forgiveness. I believe this was not only part of the plan for my salvation but part of the plan for me to be a conduit of the greatness of God to others. When I allow the blockage of unforgiveness to remain, I effectively cut off the flow of God's power in my life. Think about it. He forgave me and saved me. I am created in His image for good works in His kingdom...so if I want to be like Him, I had better learn how to be a good forgiver! The greatness of God is hindered by my resentment.

Unforgiveness builds a dam to the flow of God. Jesus sets us free, but we put ourselves back in prison when we choose to not forgive. Think about this as you read the following passage of scripture:

"Therefore, the kingdom of heaven is like a king who wanted to settle accounts with his servants. As he began the settlement, a man who owed him ten thousand bags of gold was brought to him. Since he was not able to pay, the master ordered that he and his wife and his children and all that he had be sold to repay the debt.

"At this the servant fell on his knees before him. 'Be patient with me,' he begged, 'and I will pay back everything.' The servant's master took pity on him, canceled the debt and let him go.

"But when that servant went out, he found one of his fellow servants who owed him a hundred silver coins. He grabbed him and began to choke him. 'Pay back what you owe me!' he demanded.

"His fellow servant fell to his knees and begged him, 'Be patient with me, and I will pay you back.'

"But he refused. Instead, he went off and had the man thrown into prison until he could pay the debt. When the other servants

saw what had happened, they were greatly distressed and went and told their master everything that had happened.

"Then the master called the servant in. 'You wicked servant,' he said, 'I canceled all that debt of yours because you begged me to. Shouldn't you have had mercy on your fellow servant just as I had on you?' In anger his master turned him over to the jailers to be tortured, until he should pay back all he owed.

"This is how my heavenly Father will treat each of you unless you forgive your brother from your heart." —Jesus (Matthew 18:23-35 NIV)

Another scriptural principle we can apply to the need to forgive is this: we reap what we sow; if we do not forgive, we will not receive forgiveness from others.

Forgive us our debts,
as we also have forgiven our debtors.
And lead us not into temptation,
but deliver us from the evil one.'
For if you forgive men when they sin against you, your heavenly Father will also forgive you.
But if you do not forgive men their sins, your Father will not forgive your sins. (Matthew 6:12-15 NIV)

You reap what you sow
Sow for yourselves righteousness,
reap the fruit of unfailing love,
and break up your unplowed ground;
for it is time to seek the Lord,
until he comes
and showers righteousness on you. (Hosea 10:12 NIV)

You reap what you sow.

Remember this: Whoever sows sparingly will also reap sparingly, and whoever sows generously will also reap generously. (2 Corinthians 9:6 NIV)

You reap what you sow.

Do not be deceived: God cannot be mocked.
A man reaps what he sows.
The one who sows to please his sinful nature,
from that nature will reap destruction;
the one who sows to please the Spirit,
from the Spirit will reap eternal life.
Let us not become weary in doing good,
for at the proper time we will reap a harvest if we do not give up.
(Galatians 6:7-9 NIV)

Quite simply put, when we do not forgive—when we continually bring up old offenses—we cut off the flow of God and we put ourselves right back in that mental prison where all we know is constant agony and despair. Do we really want to live there?

5. Clear Conscience Benefit

For far too many years, I could not move on with my healing because I could not forgive myself! Just as we forgive others, we must forgive ourselves or we will never move on to the deeper places in God or have that abundant life we talk so much about. To not forgive one's self is to put yourself in the place of God. To not forgive yourself is not lofty spirituality. It is pride and misinterpretation of God's forgiveness. To not forgive yourself is to place yourself on the throne of your heart...and you effectively cut off the flow of God in your life. To not forgive one's self is to say to God, "I know better than you! My standards are higher than yours!" And that, my friend, is dangerous ground to walk.

One of the greatest benefits of forgiving others is a clear conscience. Think about it. Wouldn't it be great to walk around with a clear conscience, able to hold our heads up high in the sheer joy of that freedom...to be able to look people right in the eye due to the fact that we have absolutely nothing to hide? God

God forgave me. I must humble myself to receive that forgiveness... and I must humble myself to forgive myself!

I love to read of scriptural examples of men who were able to walk in a clear conscience. Paul the apostle, while standing before the elders, chief priest, and governor said this:

So I strive always to keep my conscience clear before God and man. (Acts 24:16 NIV)
God's Word also says this about a clear conscience:
Let us draw near to God with a sincere heart
in full assurance of faith, having our hearts
sprinkled to cleanse us from a guilty conscience
and having our bodies washed with pure water.
Let us hold unswervingly to the hope we profess,
for he who promised is faithful.
And let us consider how we may spur one
another on toward love and good deeds. (Hebrews 10:22-24 NIV)

One very important aspects of forgiveness and maintaining a clear conscience is that not only should we forgive those who have offended us, but we must seek forgiveness from those we have offended. While this is not ever the most pleasant thing to have to do, it is one of the most healing things we can do for others. Look at what God's Word says about this:

"Therefore, if you are offering your gift at the altar and there remember that your brother has something against you, leave your gift there in front of the altar. First go and be reconciled to them; then come and offer your gift.

"Settle matters quickly with your adversary who is taking you to court. Do it while you are still with him on the way, or he may hand you over to the judge, and the judge may hand you over to the officer, and you may be thrown into prison. Truly I tell you, you will not get out until you have paid the last penny." —Jesus (Matthew 5:23-26 NIV)

One more thing: Be careful and don't ask someone to forgive you if they have no idea you held them in contempt. Be careful and do not direct your need to seek forgiveness at the wrong person. Here is a case in point from my own life: "Dennis, I've never struggled with same sex attraction as a Christian, and as a result, I used to hate you for your past. Please forgive me for hating you." All I hear in those words is, *I used to hate you.* Such thoughts simmer in my mind needlessly as I wonder if others in the church feel the same way. Why put someone through that torment? Deal with your sin and leave others out of it if it would lead them to wrong thoughts.

Another one I've heard: "Dennis, I was really upset at the way you led worship for a long time. Please forgive me for talking about you behind your back." All I hear is, *I and a lot of others talk about you in derogatory ways.* My thoughts immediately go to, *if he is saying those things, then others are as well.* Wouldn't it have been better to go to the ones you had talked to behind my back rather than fill my head with thoughts of self-doubt and confusion? I'm just saying that sometimes our need to seek forgiveness is directed at the wrong person.

Maybe it would be better to go to those to whom you spread your offensive attitudes to and seek their forgiveness rather than dragging another person into the mess who never even knew your wrong attitude existed. When people have approached me with things that I was never offended by, it gives the enemy a place to attack me. For that reason, let's be careful and not seek forgiveness from someone just to appease our guilty conscience if it would do more harm than good.

Here are a few questions for meditation that you may find helpful in leaving the wreckage of your resentment behind:

- Who do you need to forgive?

- Are there any areas of your life that you need to seek forgiveness from the Lord?

- Are there any areas of your own life in which you have not forgiven yourself?

- What people have you offended that you need to seek forgiveness from?

In conclusion, I simply urge you to let go of the wreckage of resentment and seek the Great Physician for your healing. Let go and move on. It is in the letting go that you will discover more of that abundant life you have dreamed of...more than you even realized you were missing...more than you realized was even possible in this life. Forgive, and watch yourself come alive.

20

THE MERRY-GO-ROUND

W hen I was a boy, the school I attended had one of those old-fashioned merry-go-rounds. Being a small town, very rural in nature, we did not have a wide variety of playground choices: swings, monkey bars, and that merry-go-round. Of course, every child wanted to ride the merry-go-round simply because of the thrill of the ride. Many were my day-dreamed reveries as I hurried through my classwork so I could envision how I would be able to get to the door before any of the other children once the teacher dismissed us for morning recess—imagining my perfect timing as I leapt from the ground to the floor of the apparatus and claiming my prized place right smack-dab in the middle.

Once the ride was fully occupied, those left waiting for their turn would summarily begin the task of putting said ride in motion. The sheer exhilaration of the experience filled my heart with joy as the wind whipped against my face and the world spun wildly around me. Utter joy. The only problem came when some of the older boys would see us younger children having a bit too much fun in their estimation and decided to make the ride more interesting. I dreaded those moments when the older antagonists would push wildly and relentlessly, faster and faster, mocking the once-joyful children whose faces now spoke sheer dread. We begged to get off as the older boys kept spinning and laughing and mocking as they chided us to go ahead and jump.

Of course, their main goal was to humiliate us to such a degree that we either risked being thrown from the merry-go-round or risked throwing ourselves from the spinning no-longer-joy-ride. Being in the middle was the safest place from my past experiences on the playground ride. Having been thrown and having jumped in past days, I had suffered scraped elbows and knees and a bruised side and ego. I surmised that being in the middle would cause the least damage. Man, was I ever wrong!

Even though I had experienced physical injury and held on for dear life in utter fear in past merry-go-round rides, being in the middle did not afford me any less pain or humiliation or fear. When one is reduced to reacting to life out of fear—regardless of where they are on the ride—the result is always the same. Even though I was not scraped or bruised in the middle, I did become hopelessly nauseous and dizzy—and afraid. The result? Puking all over myself and everyone else in the vicinity, giving the older boys all the satisfaction they had hoped for. From that day forward, I decided that to avoid the pain and suffering and humiliation and fear, I would simply get off the merry-go-round next time I saw the older boys headed my way. And guess what? The pain and suffering and humiliation and fear were suddenly non-existent!

Our thought-life is a lot like being on a merry-go-round if you think about it. For far too many years, my mind was sent into a constant spin due to the lies I believed about God and about myself. It never occurred to me that I could simply choose to get off the merry-go-round! That is our enemy's scheme. He plants a thought—a lie—into our mind, and then gives it a big old push, allowing our own fear to keep us glued to the ride. Unlike those older boys who pushed and pushed that playground version, the Liar has but to plant and push the lie into our thought patterns—and we often do the work for him. My personal belief is that the liar is not omnipresent like our God. He cannot be everywhere at once. He knows that we humans, in our pride and in our fear of what others think of us, will do his dirty work for him! He walks away and allows us to keep pushing our own merry-go-rounds of stinkin' thinkin' while he goes on to torment someone else.

So how do we get off the ride of our stinkin' thinkin'? Quite simply: get off the dang merry-go-round! Stop the stinkin' thinkin'! Renounce the lies. Replace the lies with Truth and fill your mind with

God's Word—Truth. Surround yourself with people who will love you and speak Truth to you. Speak Truth to your own mind, regardless of how you feel. Otherwise, stay on the merry-go-round and keep getting the same results: pain, sorrow, suffering, despair, self-pity, depression, and whatever the lies lead you to. It's your choice. It really is.